Looking Forward to Eternity With A Smile On My Face
Cheryl C. Conway

AGD Publishing Services, LLC

AGD Publishing Services, LLC

Copyright © 2024 By Cheryl C. Conway

All rights reserved. Under International Copyright Law, no part of this book may be reproduced, distributed, or transmitted in any form by any means: graphic, electronic, or mechanical, including photocopy, recording, taping, or by any information storage or retrieval system, without permission in writing from the author except in the case of reprints in the context of the reviews, quotes, or references.

Unless otherwise indicated, scripture quotations are from the Holy Bible, New King James Version. All rights reserved.

Printed in the United States of America

For details, Email: allisongdaniels@verizon.net
Or visit us at www.allisongdaniels.com

Cover Design:
Interior Layout: Tywebbin Creations
Editor: Sheila Hightower

Contents

DEDICATION	VII
FOREWORD	IX
INTRODUCTION	XIII
PROLOGUE "Sweet Desperation"	1
CHAPTER ONE "The Call"	5
CHAPTER TWO "Just Like You!"	11
CHAPTER THREE "All Glory To..."	15
CHAPTER FOUR "You Can't Have it Both Ways."	21
CHAPTER FIVE "You're With Me"	25
CHAPTER SIX "I'm Way Too Busy!"	29

CHAPTER SEVEN   35
"Tell Me How Did You Feel When You Come Out
De Wilderness?"

CHAPTER EIGHT   41
"Old People! What do You See in Them?"

CHAPTER NINE   45
"An Unlikely Ally – Arachnophobia"

CHAPTER TEN   49
"There Once Was a Tree"

CHAPTER ELEVEN   53
"Poor Purcell"

CHAPTER TWELVE   57
"Pruning"

CHAPTER THIRTEEN   61
"Not My Love, But Thine, Oh Lord"

CHAPTER FOURTEEN   67
"That's It!"

CHAPTER FIFTEEN   69
"A Simple Prayer"

CHAPTER SIXTEEN   73
"You Can Run, But You Can't Hide"

CHAPTER SEVENTEEN   77
"Focus on What I Do Right."

CHAPTER EIGHTEEN "Love THAT Neighbor!"??	81
CHAPTER NINETEEN "The Most Important Part"	87
CHAPTER TWENTY "Tell Them About Me"	91
CHAPTER TWENTY-ONE "COVID WOES"	95
CHAPTER TWENTY-TWO "Persimmons"	99
CHAPTER TWENTY-THREE "Snap, Crackle and Pop"!	103
CHAPTER TWENTY-FOUR "Ain't Nobody Got Time for That!"	109
CHAPTER TWENTY-FIVE "Left Behind"	115
CONCLUSION "An Uphill Climb to The. . ."	119
ADDENDUM "Hearing His Voice"	123

DEDICATION

Frances Elizabeth Woolfolk Chisley
May 4, 1916 - December 2, 1987

She never wrote a book or taught a class.
She simply lived and loved.

She was all the things I wanted to be.
Gentle, loving, peaceful,
humble, and giving.

Generous, not self-seeking, delighted and delightful,
Tender yet strong. Soft-spoken with an infectious laugh.

Devoted and patient.
Comforting and caring.
Supportive and sacrificial.
Deserving, yet undemanding.
Understanding and available.

Beautiful inside and out.

Happy Heavenly Birthday Mom!
Looking forward to seeing you again
and hearing you call my name. 🖤

FOREWORD

Dear Friend,

The Lord had me to pray for you this morning. I prayed that He would give me the words to say to you so that your heart could hear. When I finished, I felt led to write this.

I have personally experienced and I, even now, am experiencing an ongoing personal relationship with Jesus. I feel cherished and protected. I feel understood and known. Beyond anything I've ever experienced with any person, including my parents, my husband, my family, and friends – no other relationship has ever or will ever come close. To be truly known inside out, even my faults and my struggles, and yet to be fully accepted, is most precious. Jesus loves the world - which is why He suffered, gave His life, and died a cruel death for us all. He demonstrated this incomprehensible love to me in an instant when I asked Him, why He did what He did for people like me and all the sinners in the world? In answer to my question, for a brief instant, He allowed me to experience an immense expansion of my heart -

graphically demonstrating His love for the entire world - every person.

In that instant, I was totally and eternally convinced that Jesus is who He said He was – the Savior of the world who was sent and willingly came out of the great love He has for all of us. He did not come down from Heaven to suffer on earth for a few, or just for specific groupings, but for everybody. His desire is that none should perish but that all would be saved. He told His disciples to go into all the world to make disciples of all men. Jesus is not exclusive –He is inclusive. He is totally and awesomely loving. Jesus is the epitome and the personification of the love of God. He demonstrated that to me personally. Yes, Jesus loves us.

When I am in distress I can speak to Him in my prayer closet - or wherever I am, and He answers me. He comforts me, reassures me, and He corrects me when I need it. I hear His voice in my spirit. Sometimes He speaks to me before I even call Him or even speak His name. He sees my distress and reassures me, *"I am here."* I know that I'm beloved of Him. I know that He only wants the best for my life – but will allow me to experience those things that change me for my good and for the good of others. He's gentle, all wise, and all loving.

There are times when I might have difficulty understanding all the precepts and teachings of the Bible, but what I know beyond a shadow of doubt is that

Jesus is real, He is alive, He is actively involved on behalf of all people, and He is completely trustworthy. And yet, He is not merely the perfect lover of our souls; He's all powerful and He is the one who will judge us all. And because of Jesus' great sacrifice for us, we can be made right with God when we receive Him into our hearts as our Savior and Lord. God is not going to set that aside lightly. Jesus is God's precious Son sent to give us His love and forgiveness of our sins. Through Jesus, God has created a unique pathway whereby we can come to Him while here on the earth and then spend eternity with Him. If we reject the Father's great gift, Jesus, how can we be reconciled with God?

We are all sinners and can only be made acceptable to spend eternity with our Holy God - not by our good works or our good deeds - but by the spiritual cleansing and regeneration we can only receive by trusting Jesus as Savior and Lord of our lives. I wonder if you can imagine sending your son, your only son, to suffer and die for people who then refused to honor His sacrifice? Imagine God saying, *My Beloved world, I see that you are struggling in sin. I know that you can't be free and stay free on your own. So I'm sending you My most precious gift - My Son - who will die for you and live in you. Through Him you can be restored to Me and have an abundant life of joy and peace. He is all you need. Just open your heart to Him.*

Many people may love us, dear friend, but only Jesus can love us perfectly. No "religion" can take the place of a personal relationship with a personal savior. Our hearts need Him. Yes, our wounded hearts need to be healed by the love that only He can provide.

Love,

Cheryl

P.S. After writing this, the lyrics of the 1963 Motown hit "Heat Wave", by Holland–Dozier–Holland came to my mind. I wonder who remembers it:

"I can't explain it, don't understand it, I ain't never felt like this before! Yeah, that funny feelings got me amazed – don't know what to do, my head is in a haze – it's like a heat wave!"

That's where I'm coming from! Jesus is the perfect love we have all been longing for –searching for.

J E S U S, The True and immortal lover of our souls!

INTRODUCTION

Conceived by the Holy Spirit in 2013, the chapters of this book represent a journey of intimacy with the Master of the Universe, the Lord of All, the Majestic Mighty King, The Holy Lamb of God, The Great I AM, my Very Best Friend and Closest Confidante, the Lover of My Soul, My Heavenly Husband, Jesus the Christ! I believe that His desire in commissioning this book was to draw His people into a closer relationship with Him.

My assignment was to "Write About My Struggles and God's Goodness." I have been required to remove the mask and reveal some of the ungodly actions, attitudes, and thoughts that the Lord is continuing to help me to overcome as I follow Him. In contrast to my imperfections, His goodness shines all the brighter!

I pray that somewhere in this book, something I have shared will possibly help you in your journey. As we look back over our lives, the details will differ, but the message is the same:

HE LOVES US, and desires intimacy with us even in our imperfection. His love can penetrate all the layers of self-protection, selfishness, and selfish ambition that often weigh us down. He knows our *true* identity and He will work tirelessly to free us to walk in that truth. Our destiny is dependent on allowing Him to commune with us in our hearts and bring His healing touch to our woundedness. Those of us who have trusted Him to do so have begun a wonderful journey beyond our wildest and fondest imagination! Our Beloved Lord beckons His beloved, you, me. Won't you follow?

All GLORY TO GOD! For HE has done MARVELOUS THINGS!!

PROLOGUE
"Sweet Desperation"

> *O God, You are my God;*
> *Early will I seek You;*
> *My soul thirsts for You;*
> *My flesh longs for You*
> *In a dry and thirsty land*
> *Where there is no water."*
> *– Psalm 63:1*

On the last day of a five-day fast, I was so looking forward to my meal - delicious, broiled chicken, sweet potatoes, and collard greens! And maybe a piece of pie for dessert! I told the Lord that I would break it at 3:00 p.m. (*Perhaps my first mistake...*) As the minutes ticked slowly by, I found myself growing impatient. Would it ever be time to eat? I began to feel weak and slightly faint as a sense of desperation began to take over. Would 3:00 p.m ever come?

At 2:45 p.m., I heard the Holy Spirit say, "5:00 p.m." I couldn't believe my ears! Hadn't I been faithful for the last five days? As much as I wanted to think that I had heard wrong, I knew that I had heard correctly and that I had to wait TWO MORE HOURS before I could eat! As I was bemoaning my fate, I heard the Lord Jesus say in my spirit, "***I don't want you to be desperate for anything except Me.***"

All my desperation was replaced by sweet contentment - a contentment that only Jesus could provide. All I could say, all I wanted to say was, "Yes, Lord!" This is the Savior that I love so much! Only He can turn panic into such a deep sense of peace and satisfaction.

I don't want to downplay His holiness, His majesty, or His power. I don't want to downplay His authority or His sovereignty. All these aspects of our Lord are awe-inspiring and create a deep sense of reverence. But this and many other encounters demonstrate His passionate and personal love for us. They prove that He is paying close attention, that He understands all our needs, and that He can fill them like no one else can. This encounter speaks to relationship – to closeness, a knitting together of hearts. He knew that though it was natural for me to be physically hungry at that point, my *critical* need was for my spiritual hunger to be reignited. So, He stepped in and reclaimed that which should only belong to Him.

My heart is moved to reflect the lyrics of the beautiful worship song, "Seated at the Right Hand of God" on Tye

Tribbett's Victory Live! Album, "Who would not serve a God like Him? I bow right now." Yes, Lord, I bow right now.

It's because of who our incomparable Lord Jesus reveals Himself to be toward us at moments like this that I am truly **looking forward to eternity with a big smile on my face!**

> "I know your works, that you are neither cold nor hot. I could wish you were cold or hot. So then, because you are lukewarm, and neither cold nor hot, I will vomit you out of My mouth."
> – *Revelation 3:15-16*

CHAPTER ONE

"The Call"

> *"... that you may proclaim the praises of Him who called you out of darkness into His marvelous light;"*
> *– 1 Peter 2:9*

While 'working from home,' I found it most difficult to make the best use of my time. My worship CD had just been released and my husband and I had participated in a few discussions with our producer and other respected friends to discuss promoting the music. Unfortunately, those meetings had resulted in more questions than answers, leaving me conflicted about how to proceed with the ministry the Lord had given birth to.

The Lord had communicated the CD assignment to me one Sunday morning while I was singing with our church's praise and worship team. He spoke the phrase ***"Worship CD"*** into my spirit. About a year later, I received confirmation during another church service, after which I began to take the first steps to do something I had never done or even imagined myself doing. I stepped out in faith.

In faith I sought the Lord for the songs, and He began to awaken me night after night with the outpouring of original lyrics and melodies. His visions in my dreams confirmed His chosen producer. Seven years later, while ministering at my CD release concert, I felt that I had been created for this – to draw God's people closer to Him through music. The project was completed, and I was entirely on board and ready to move and charge ahead!

The Lord had said that He would promote me. Of course, I desired to be in His will, but I wondered what I should be doing now. On the one hand, I considered the advice of those we consulted about the next steps - hiring a marketing expert, making personal announcements on social media platforms, contacting radio stations, and recording music videos. But, on the other hand, I felt my usual discomfort or uneasiness about promoting myself. Perhaps I should wait for the Lord to open the right doors at the right time?

So here I was, trapped in a whirlwind of approach/avoidance responses. Directly after the release concert, the Lord had merely instructed, **"Keep your voice strong,"** but I was chomping at the bit to move forward quickly! Not knowing what to do, I had spent most of the previous day (and many others) watching

TV, web surfing, and playing games on my IPAD that are self-described as 'time killers.' Hmmm…

So, this morning, when I quietly asked The Lord to help me structure my day, I heard His *'still, small voice'* (1 Kings 19:12) say to me, **"Write a book about My goodness."**

How delightful! I didn't find this new assignment shocking even though I had never written a book. In fact, like the worship CD, I had never even considered doing so. The Lord had seen me through the entire CD process, so why should this be any different? So, what if my vision seemed to be failing? (*No doubt due to all the TV/computer/IPad viewing*). My history with God demonstrated that these things we see as obstacles are nothing to Him. I was excited to begin, and now that I had watched and wept over every episode of the CBS reruns of "Judging Amy," His timing seemed perfect - as always!

As I considered how I would write about His goodness, I thought of "Abba Calling" by Charles Slagle, one of my favorite daily devotionals. It reveals the very heart of Our Heavenly Father on every page: so personal - so intimate.

I have experienced His love in many different and personal ways. He wants that for all His children. As we open our hearts to Him, He will commune with us Spirit-to-spirit, invariably hitting the target of our every need with laser-beam accuracy! His heart and mind are so loving and beautiful, and He speaks on such a profound level that it invariably makes my heart dance with delight! In this world of duplicity and hidden agendas, His absolute truth has a way of doing that. His words are like manna to my weary soul. I have tasted and seen that the Lord is truly good. (*Psalm 34:8*, "**Oh, taste and see that the Lord is good; Blessed is the man who trusts in Him**")

As I contemplated this exciting new assignment, the Lord clarified the assignment further by specifying that He wanted the book to be about "***my struggles* and His goodness.**" Oh oh...

His goodness is one of my favorite subjects. But I also must expose my weaknesses and flaws in this book. I was being asked to remove the mask of Christian perfection and reveal the inward mess I often struggle with. The shedding of pretense would necessitate a higher degree of trust. I felt like Apostle Peter, being invited to step out into deep, dangerous waters with Jesus. I feared that exposing my personal flaws might open me up to ridicule or even disdain.

As I considered the *required* transparency, the faces of some of my "church friends" flashed into my mind. My friends from outside the church knew and shared various degrees of my "stinking thinking," but my church friends appeared to be perfect. Their demeanor seemed to confirm my erroneous belief that we are all supposed to be immediately perfected when we receive salvation. I realized I wasn't, which worried me, but I was playing the part to the hilt! I thought to myself, *'How would they respond when they knew what was happening on the inside of me while I appeared to have it all together?'* I had to take a moment to "count the cost" (*Luke 14:28,* "**For which of you, intending to build a tower, does not sit down first and count the cost, whether he has enough to finish it—.**"*)* But then I considered that it was Jesus making the request - the One who has given His all for me. I knew that The One who was asking is entirely trustworthy and always looking out for the good of all. And because it was Him asking, I chose to accept the invitation. And here I stand willing and ready to, ever-so-gently, peel back the mask...

> "**Trust in the Lord with all thine heart; and lean not unto thine own understanding. In all thy ways acknowledge him, and he shall direct thy paths.**"
> – *Proverbs 3:5-6 (KJV)*

CHAPTER TWO

"Just Like You!"

> *"Now may the God of peace Himself sanctify you completely; and may your whole spirit, soul, and body be preserved blameless at the coming of our Lord Jesus Christ. He who calls you is faithful, who also will do it."*
> *– 1 Thessalonians 5:23-24*

I stood alone in the kitchen early that Christmas morning. In the quiet stillness, I gazed upon the soft coral and garnet colors of the adjoining dining room walls and draperies as the morning sun cast a delicate glow over the newly decorated space. I saw the table's polished wood, the well-loved family piano, and the rich tones of the gleaming hardwood floors. My coordinated Christmas garland adorned the doorway.

"Beautiful!" I thought. Then my eyes fell on the floor in my kitchen that was in dire need of repair. The laminate had peeled off entirely in several places, and there were wide gaps between the planks that I had carefully tried to conceal with festive red throw rugs. "...but imperfect,"

I concluded. As soon as the thought came into my mind, I heard the Lord's still, small voice say, *"Just like you."*

Beloved friends, it would be an understatement to say that I was deeply moved. This was one of the first times I had clearly recognized the Lord's voice. As I thought about what He had said, I conveniently overlooked the "but imperfect" part and focused entirely on "Beautiful!" It was a classic case of a person only hearing what they want to hear. It didn't occur to me that He spoke of *internal* rather than external beauty. In my mind, the Lord, who is the Way, the **Truth**, and the Life (John 14:6), had called me beautiful, and off I rushed to the nearest mirror to try to see myself through His eyes!

Failing in that effort, I began to reflect soberly on His meaning. The Lord had spoken volumes with just a few simple words. The condition of my house reflected the condition of my heart. In His all-seeing eyes, I was "beautiful BUT imperfect." I needed remodeling, and He was the One who would be doing it. He was not only saying, "I love you just as you are," but He was also saying, "I love you too much to let you stay as you are."

Just as there were gaps between the kitchen floor planks, there were gaps in my heart that needed to be filled in. Moreover, there were entire planks that needed to be replaced. And before the work could commence, the red throw rugs must first be removed - no more hiding and no more covering up the flaws. The Master

Carpenter would rebuild me with new, perfect, and eternal materials! To God be the glory, and what a tremendous comfort to know that He has never left a project unfinished!

His divine renovation project has continued since that insightful Christmas morning. It hasn't always been easy, and at times I have resisted His efforts. It's been difficult to relinquish the faulty defense mechanisms I had developed over the course of my life. After struggling through painful childhood trauma and family dysfunction, the crutches of pride and anger had grown to feel like familiar, reliable friends.

During one time of resistance, I acknowledged to Jesus, *"After all You've done for me, You shouldn't have to work so hard to convince me to trust You."* He lovingly responded, **"Whatever it takes."** I was reminded once again of His utter devotion and patient persistence, so my stubborn heart yielded. I willingly submitted to the One and Only One who loves me thoroughly, knows exactly what I need, and has the unique power to transform me into His beautiful likeness. And over the years, He has proven time and time again that what He has to give me is infinitely better than whatever He may be coaxing me to let go of and give up.

"being confident of this very thing, that He who has begun a good work in you will

complete it until the day of Jesus Christ;"
– Philippians 1:6

CHAPTER THREE

"All Glory To..."

> *"The king spoke, saying, "Is not this great Babylon, that I have built for a royal dwelling by my mighty power and for the honor of my majesty?" While the word was still in the king's mouth, a voice fell from heaven: "King Nebuchadnezzar, to you it is spoken: the kingdom has departed from you! And they shall drive you from men, and your dwelling shall be with the beasts of the field. They shall make you eat grass like oxen; and seven times shall pass over you, until you know that the Most High rules in the kingdom of men, and gives it to whomever He chooses." That very hour the word was fulfilled concerning Nebuchadnezzar; he was driven from men and ate grass like oxen; his body was wet with the dew of heaven till his hair had grown like eagles' feathers and his nails like birds' claws." – Daniel 4:30-33*

Growing up, I received a lot of praise, primarily for my academic accomplishments.

Learning has always been easy for me. I graduated as valedictorian of my high school class and made the dean's list in my first college semester. (As for the other semesters...well, I felt that I had proved my point, and the Bid Whist games in the student lounge were so much more inviting than my homework!) I never gave these things much thought. I took it all for granted - the achievements and the accolades.

Fast forward twenty-five years, and as a new follower of Christ, I learned that praise and glory are not for me but should only be given to the Lord. That was a major paradigm shift! Having given you the background, beloved reader, I feel safe making this confession: I became a glory seeker.

I loved receiving the credit when I said or did something right, and it was difficult to resist saying, "I told you so." when I was proven right. I wanted the kudos, the congratulations, the applause. I craved it –I craved it all. If I sang a song well or ministered a dance well on any given Sunday, I wanted everyone to still be talking about it when we came back to church the following Sunday! I know this might surprise those of you who know me, but, it's nonetheless true. I tried to keep all my foolishness under wraps. I truly tried to follow the blueprint for proper Christian behavior. Still, eventually, I had to learn the hard way -- not to take God's glory.

One Sunday afternoon, our dance ministry was invited to minister at a sister church. At the time our ministry had three components who ministered separately.

There were also a few other groups and dancers from other churches - notably one young lady who did a beautiful solo dance. My group danced last, and the response was overwhelming. Our ministry elicited loud praises from the congregation. I remember seeing it as a personal victory as I had choreographed and taught the dance. (In my heart, we were in competition with the other adult groups and had clearly won. Just keeping it real...)

As we left the sanctuary, I passed the young lady who had danced so beautifully and complimented her. She looked me in the eye and said, "To God be the glory." I thought, "Hmm. That's strange. She doesn't seem happy that her gifts and talents are being recognized. I'll try again." So, I repeated myself, and she repeated herself with the same direct look into my eyes, "To God be the glory." Never one to be easily deterred, I tried again and received the same response.

I felt a little strange but decided to shake it off and just continued to enjoy basking in my own personal glory. I went into the dressing room with my mature sisters but kept my personal feelings under wraps as we changed out of our dance garments. All was still going swimmingly well, and I was still flying high! However, upon leaving the building, I was confronted with the scene of a very loving member of our church who seemed to be in a great deal of distress. She was surrounded by many of our members. It crossed my mind to go over and lend support, but shamefully I decided I was enjoying this glory thing so much that I didn't want to get involved. I justified it by thinking that she had plenty of help around her.

On I swaggered, happy as a lark, until I turned the corner to go to the rear parking lot. The best way to describe what happened next is that it was as if a pack of heavy monkeys had suddenly jumped on my back. Gone was the elation from the applause and recognition. Instead, I felt a heavy, oppressive presence in my spirit that weighed me down and caused fear, sadness, guilt, and shame.

I made it to my car but was barely able to drive off because of the state of my emotions. I wept bitterly the whole way home and cried every day for the next week. I couldn't escape the remorse and shame of mistreating this precious sister. I implored God to free me from this agony. I called her to confess my betrayal and asked for forgiveness. Despite, and maybe because of her graciousness, I can't imagine Judas Iscariot feeling worse!

There was no relief until I returned to church the following Sunday. As we joined hands in a circle and our Sunday School teacher prayed, I was suddenly bent over at the waist by an unseen force. Our teacher said it was like an angel of the Lord had streaked down from heaven and into our circle. I arose, freed from the torment of the past week! Hallelujah, and to GOD be the GLORY!!!

Proverbs 3:11-12 says, **"My son, do not despise the chastening of the Lord, nor detest His correction; For whom the Lord loves He corrects, Just as a father the son in whom he delights."** Precious reader, I praise God for this lesson. I believe He tried to warn me through the young dancer, but when I ignored the warning, He taught me in a way I will never forget. ALL glory belongs to God! He alone is worthy of praise!!!

This is not to say that I still don't crave it (the glory) sometimes. I have confessed my desire to Jesus. His response? ***"I know, but that makes it all the more precious when you give it to Me."***

THIS is MY Savior! THIS is MY Lord! ♥♥♥

JESUS, HOW BEAUTIFUL YOU ARE!!!

"But 'he who glories, let him glory in the Lord.' For not he who commends himself is approved, but whom the Lord commends."
– *2 Corinthians 10:17-18 (KJV)*

CHAPTER FOUR

"You Can't Have it Both Ways."

> *"For if you forgive men their trespasses, your heavenly Father will also forgive you. But if you do not forgive men their trespasses, neither will your Father forgive your trespasses."*
> *– Matthew 6:14-15*

It's not always easy being a Christian. When we receive Christ and all the benefits of a personal relationship with the God of the universe, we must give some things up. For instance, we must give up our natural tendency to act out of our hurt and respond in like-kind to wounds that have been inflicted upon us. When someone offends us, our natural response is to withdraw from the relationship and/or to get even.

We may feel stronger and more protected when we take these approaches, but are we? When we surrender our lives to Christ, shouldn't we trust Him to protect us? *2 Thessalonians 3:3* says, **"But the Lord is faithful, who will establish you and guard you from the evil one."** Shouldn't we allow the Lord to let us know which relationships He wants for us?

Perhaps God connected you in the relationship because the person needs to have a deeper connection with you to grow in their walk? And maybe you need to have a deeper connection with them to grow in your walk? What is God saying about it? I suggest that it behooves us to seriously consider that this might be a God-ordained relationship that the enemy tried to sabotage by orchestrating the scenario that caused us to be wounded.

And of course, we know that forgiveness is always required whatever the person has done or not done. We must forgive. And when we consider Jesus' response to Peter's request about forgiveness in *Matthew 18:22*, we realize that keeping track of wrongs is a fruitless effort if we are to be true disciples of our Lord. He says we must forgive **"seventy times seven times,"** and who can keep track of that!

I thought I had learned this lesson, but on the last days of December 2019, I discovered that I needed a refresher course.

Wherever I went I felt an oppressive heaviness in my spirit. And even though I had gone through the motions of saying that I forgave the person who had once again hurt me, I continued to feel weighed down. Every time the offense came to mind, I felt the wound re-open. I had been able to forgive him in the past, but this time it was much harder. Perhaps I had reached my personal limit...

As I prayed for relief, the Lord brought the unforgiveness to my mind and said, ***"You can't have it both ways, Cheryl."*** You see, I was trying to walk in His peace and joy while still nursing my wounds and holding the perpetrator accountable. My efforts to escape the heaviness were to no avail. I was powerless because of my unforgiveness. I had to choose between remaining on my self-made throne of "righteous indignation" or walking in God's peace.

The Lord showed His mercy by allowing unshakeable heaviness to force me to my knees. As painful as the offense had been, continuing to dwell in unforgiveness was proving to be much worse.

So, I made the heartfelt decision to choose to truly forgive, and I left the repair of my emotions in the Lord's hands. It didn't happen overnight, but as I continued to choose forgiveness over bitterness, my heart did heal.

Months later the same person needed assistance and the Lord enlisted me to reach out and help. He was able to use me in that situation because I had forgiven, and no longer had bitterness in my heart.

Dear readers, let's stay useful to our Heavenly Father by choosing forgiveness, peace and joy over bitterness and resentment. Let's choose the narrow gate - our Savior's path. The days are evil and the time is short. It's more important than ever to seek to remain in God's perfect will in all matters. If we take our pain to Him, He will heal us. And if we seek Him for direction, the Lord will show us His will for the relationship. **"In all of our ways (we must) acknowledge Him, and He will direct our path."** (Proverbs 3:6)

Let's remove the limits, leave the past behind, and press towards the mark of His higher calling with open minds and healed hearts. ❤

> **"Enter by the narrow gate; for wide is the gate and broad is the way that leads to destruction, and there are many who go in by it. Because narrow is the gate and difficult is the way which leads to life, and there are few who find it."**
> *- Matthew 7:13-14*

CHAPTER FIVE
"You're With Me"

> *"Fear not, for I am with you;*
> *Be not dismayed, for I am your God.*
> *I will strengthen you,*
> *Yes, I will help you,*
> *I will uphold you with.*
> *My righteous right hand."*
> *– Isaiah 41:10*

I went alone that day to support a friend who was burying her mom. We had not been particularly close, more like casual acquaintances connected through our children's friendship. But I went to support the family and planned to leave right after the service.

I hugged her and her son as she left the sanctuary and as I was walking towards the exit I heard the Holy Spirit say, **"Stay."** Since I wasn't a member of their church, I wasn't sure how I would 'fit in.' The few other people that I knew had left. Still, since I was sure I heard the Holy Spirit's instruction, I turned towards the fellowship hall where the family and their close friends were gathering for the repast.

Standing alone at the entrance, I felt awkward and out of place. The grieving family was busy and surrounded by people in their close circle. I searched the room for a place to sit but found very few empty chairs, and the few I did see were at tables where the people all seemed to know each other. A sudden wave of social anxiety washed over me, and I immediately recalled a similar dilemma many years before at a Jr. High School dance.

I stood at the gym entrance, isolated and alone in my Bobbie Socks and saddle oxfords. I remember feeling as if a spotlight was shining on me as I nervously eyed the wide floor separating me from the cool and connected girls in their stockings and lipstick on the other side of the gym.

Many decades later, here I stood - isolated and alone. Any confidence I had gained from the intervening years had evaporated. At that moment, I felt just like that insecure girl standing in the gym doorway. Finally, I summoned all my courage, crossed the room, and approached a table with an empty chair, only to be told it was taken.

I was sorely tempted to turn on my heels and walk out of the church, but instead I returned to my lookout point in the doorway feeling deflated and even more out of place. Other people came in, looked around, found their 'person,' waved enthusiastically, and marched confidently to their reserved seats. I felt unwelcome and foolish.

Then very distinctly, I heard the Lord say, ***"You're with Me."*** Beloved reader, can I tell you how my heart rejoiced, and my fears vanished! My Knight in Shining Armor had come to my rescue! I hadn't asked, hadn't prayed, but He saw the state of my emotions and came immediately to my aid!

"You're with Me." Those three words gave me such a surge of joy and confidence. I no longer felt alone but was assured that I was in the best company imaginable. With Jesus as my divine date, I walked comfortably across the room to an empty chair I hadn't noticed before and enjoyed a delightful fellowship with the people at the table.

"The Lord is my helper; I will not fear. What can man do to me?" *(Hebrews 13:5b-6)*

This precious memory endures and assures me of His attentive, compassionate love. I am sharing it so that it can do the same for you. This relationship is the basis for our strength.

More and more these days, the Lord is marshalling His Body to take on assignments to advance His Kingdom. No matter how daunting the assignment, remembering that we are with Him will shrink it down to a manageable size. We must remember that He is not sending us out alone, but, like a child with a powerful parent, *we* are with **Him**. What do we have to fear? He won't only be standing beside us, but He is leading the charge, and clearing obstacles out of the way. He has already established the victory for us, as we follow Him. **("And the LORD, He is the One who goes before you...")** *Deuteronomy 31:8.*

Trust Him to always come to the rescue. ❤

"I will not leave you comfortless: I will come to you."
-John 14:18, KJV

CHAPTER SIX
"I'm Way Too Busy!"

> *"For I know the thoughts that I think toward you, says the Lord, thoughts of peace and not of evil, to give you a future and a hope."*
> *– Jeremiah 29:11*

"I'm sorry, Auntie. I can't be in the church play because I can't come to the Monday night rehearsals. That's one of the nights that I take my African dance class." I hoped this would seal the deal and force my dear aunt to stop asking me. *"OK, baby,"* she said, *"There's plenty of time. It's June, and the play isn't until September." "OK, Auntie,"* I replied gently, *"but I don't think anything will change." "OK, baby,"* she said. *"You have a nice day. I love you." "I love you too, Auntie. Bye-bye."*

"Phew!" I thought. *"I hope that's the last of that. I don't have time to be in that play. Besides, it sounds so boring. My life away from the church is so much more exciting."*

Mind you, precious reader, this all took place after I recovered from the deep depression, anxiety, and panic attacks I experienced ten months after we had laid my

Beloved Mom to rest. I was diagnosed with "Delayed Grief Syndrome", and I found myself unable to take care of my beautiful 14-year-old daughter or go to work. I wandered through months of unexplainable fear, confusion, hallucinations, and even suicidal thoughts punctuated by frequent emergency room visits. I was a single parent, and having never experienced mental illness, my first response was to protect Nia by sending her to stay with my brother and his family until I got better.

I was not a Believer then. I would describe myself as closer to an agnostic (skeptic). Still, during my darkest hours, I could only think to pray and recite the 23rd Psalm I learned during sporadic childhood church visits.

Thanks be to God! The Lord brought me out of it, and He delivered me entirely without the lifelong dependency on anti-anxiety medications that some doctors had suggested. I can still recall the nervous excitement I felt when Nia came back home, and we resumed our lives together. ❤

Out of gratitude and relief, I started attending church regularly for the first time. I even joined the choir, but not much else had changed with me. I was still living a worldly life, and the thought of being in a church play was unappealing. Besides, one of my doctors had prescribed vigorous physical exercise to the point of exhaustion two or three times a week as part of my recovery regimen, and it was working! I had never felt better --thanks to the hour-and-a-half African dance class I was taking three times a week.

This was all well and good, but unbeknownst to me, the Lord had not delivered me just so I could return to business as usual. Looking back, He was clearly positioning me to make a major shift in my life and He would use my aunt's tenacity to do it.

To her credit, Auntie did wait three months before popping the question again. This time it was right before the Kankouran West African Dance Company's Annual Labor Day Weekend African Dance Conference which I had been looking forward to since the prior year. Instructors and drummers came from many West African nations, and we would have the opportunity to learn new dances to new rhythms and dance with dancers from around the world. It would take place over three days with non-stop classes. As exhausting as that may sound, African dance was a great passion of my life, and the conference was one of the major highlights of my year.

So, when she asked, I was sure I had the perfect excuse. Nothing could keep me from that conference. *"Baby, what about the play? They really need someone to dance, and I think there's a song that they need a soloist for."* I quickly (but gently) responded, *"Auntie, I'm sorry. I have a major dance conference over the weekend."* ("Checkmate!" I thought. The deal would have to be sealed after the long three-month delay and my continuing unavailability this close to the production date.) But Auntie saw another move, and just as quickly responded in her sweetest voice, *"Well, what about after that, baby?"* Not to be outplayed, I replied, *"Well, Auntie, that will be too late. The play is in a few weeks, right?"* (Surely this had to do it.) *"That's OK, baby,"* she said. *"You're a quick study. Come on after your conference is over."* And with that, she had me. I had no more excuses since the dance studio closed for several weeks every year after the Labor Day Conference.

The following week I started rehearsing for Meade Memorial Episcopal Church's production of "The Clown" by Carl Mays. It wasn't as torturous as I expected as I collaborated with another young lady to choreograph and rehearse the dance. Then, one day as we stood onstage discussing the movements, I found my attention drawn to a conversation being conducted in the auditorium.

The director was sitting and laughing with a man I had never seen as they discussed something related to the play. The man was "tall, dark, and handsome," with a smile that caused my heart to skip a beat. Purcell George Conway, my wonderful husband, my forever love, and the man I would walk with through the rest of my life's journey had stepped into my life. I was to discover that this was the man God selected for me - to love me as Christ loves the Church. Hallelujah!! Thank You, Jesus!!!

But wait, there's more! The Lord had more in store for me, and I was in the right place to receive it due to my aunt's persistence. "The Clown", *A Dramatic Musical Experience of Spiritual Encounter and Christian Witness* as the playwright described it, was just that. Through the music and dialogue in that anointed play, my spiritual eyes and heart began to open for the first time.

In one of the lines in the play, an actress describes Jesus by saying, "He's real! He's so real!" It was a simple line, but it was as if a light bulb turned on for me, and for the first time, I considered that maybe He was. Until that moment, I had not given Jesus much thought as I struggled through life, looking for something or someone to fill a hole, a void I couldn't define. I believed it was a husband I needed, and my godly husband is more of a blessing than I can describe. But even more than that, I needed a loving Savior.

A seed of faith was planted via that anointed production, and the Lord saw to it that it was watered and nurtured until it came to full bloom in my heart, where it flourishes today. To God be the glory!

And special thanks to my beloved, dearly departed Auntie. I don't know why it was so important to her, but I believe that God used her as His instrument to get me into that life-changing play! I am eternally grateful. ❤

> "O taste and see that the Lord is good: blessed is the man that trusteth in him."
> – *Psalm 34:8 (KJV)*

CHAPTER SEVEN

"Tell Me How Did You Feel When You Come Out De Wilderness?"

> *"But if anyone does not provide for his own, and especially for those of his household, he has denied the faith and is worse than an unbeliever."*
> - 1 Timothy 5:8

"Tell Me How Did You Feel When You Come Out De Wilderness?" The words of this old spiritual came to mind as I began to write this chapter. Have you ever wondered why the Lord allows you to be placed in certain situations that seem to be full of dangerous temptations for you? I found myself there when we brought my aunt into our home during a time of medical distress. All my buttons were pushed repeatedly by my dear, sweet Auntie.

After a two-week hospital stay, at 105 1/2 years old, Auntie was discharged into round-the-clock home care because of a very wide and deep bedsore that was open down to the bone. My husband and I offered to bring her home with us because we were in a better position to provide the environment for round-the-clock care. Our family agreed, and thus our journey began. Medical professionals had little hope for her survival because of her age and the severity of the wound. However, the Lord confirmed His will by giving me a vision of her deep wound being completely healed and covered with fresh new skin. ***"This is a house of healing, not a house of death,"*** He declared. I had the faith to believe Him for her physical healing, but didn't anticipate the emotional and spiritual turmoil that we would soon be engulfed in.

And that is precisely where we found ourselves. We did everything we could to make her comfortable. She had home health aides providing round-the-clock care. Her wounds were healing as God had promised, but she was miserable. She found herself in unfamiliar surroundings, in an uncomfortable state, with strangers tending to her medical needs, and there was to be no peace for anyone. In her weakened physical, mental, and emotional state, dear Auntie repeated her request to go home continuously for hours on end. As the weeks turned into months, though her wound was healing and she was miraculously experiencing very little physical pain, her mental and emotional state remained the same, and her demand never ended.

Meanwhile, the enemy was working overtime on my flesh, stirring up anger, frustration, impatience, and resentment. This was a difficult assignment that brought out many negative emotions --daily. It's clear to me now that I was operating in the spirit of pride and self-righteousness. I believed that we were making an extreme sacrifice for her good, and I wanted to be appreciated. I wanted kudos for helping her, but instead I was getting complaints all day long and sometimes into the night. My compassion and patience were both stretched well beyond their limits. My aunt was the one suffering, and I wanted her to feel better, but if the truth be told, often I felt sorry for myself more than I did for her.

Don't get me wrong; I considered it an honor to care for Auntie in her struggle. She had always been a loving aunt and had sacrificed her own happiness for the good of the family. This is the same aunt the Lord had used to coax me to be in the play where I met both my husband and my Lord and Savior, Jesus. Single and childless, Auntie had outlived her siblings and had assumed the role of family matriarch. She had a big heart, a brilliant mind, and an excellent memory. She had always been a bit of a worrier and a little bossy (my daughter had affectionately nicknamed her "The General"). We all loved and appreciated her, and we were very proud of her. But now she was directing all her significant mental resources towards orchestrating her way back home prematurely.

Understandably, she desired to be back in the comfort of her own bed, but she couldn't go home until her wound had fully healed. Nevertheless, her mind was set on it, and with her characteristic tenacity, she wouldn't let it go. I found myself running out of patience - becoming frustrated and even taking offense at her unwillingness to at least attempt to be soothed by our help and assurances. The entire time she was recuperating in our home she regarded herself as stranded in an unfamiliar wilderness. And right next to her, I was struggling in my own wilderness. This was testing time.

There was nowhere to go and nothing to do to escape Auntie's strangely powerful and penetrating voice that was echoing throughout the house. Just as I was getting to the point of losing my composure, I heard the Lord whisper **"I am here."** True to His Word, He was an ever-present help in the time of trouble. He had been there all along, and made His presence known just when I needed Him the most. His nearness brought about a peace and enabled me to resist the temptation to give full vent to my frustration and indignation. His soft reminder had saved the day for all concerned.

After 7½ months Auntie's bedsore was fully healed and covered with fresh new skin as God had promised. She was finally able to return to her beloved family home where she flourished well past the age of 109. By the power, love, and guidance of the Lord, we had both made it out of the wilderness!

"My brethren, count it all joy when you fall into various trials, knowing that the testing of your faith produces patience. But let patience have its perfect work, that you may be perfect and complete, lacking nothing."
-James 1:2-4

CHAPTER EIGHT

"Old People! What do You See in Them?"

> *"Do not cast me off in the time of old age;*
> *Do not forsake me when my strength fails."*
> - Psalm 71:9

A wistful expression came over my friend's face as she lovingly said, *"I really love old people."* In my shock I blurted out, *"Old people"?? What do you see in them?!?!"* Now, before you condemn me dear reader for being an insensitive gerontophobia (a person who has a fear of, disdain for, or aversion to old people,) hear me out. This was decades before I became a Believer, and I simply could not understand her fascination with the elderly. In my unredeemed mind, I felt that there were so many more interesting people in the world - ones with full use of their bodies and mental faculties.

My friend was a Believer. Over the years her heart had been tenderized by the Holy Spirit, and though we had many other things in common, that was where we parted ways. My only Christian friend, Joan never tried to convert me, and her one attempt at saving my soul was to advise me very seriously one day to never take a mark on my hand or forehead. Of course, this was meaningless to me at the time, but her somber demeanor got my attention, making that remark stand out in my memory among the thousands of conversations we had. I know now what it took for her to bring it up, and I will always love her for it. But I digress...

In answer to my question, she went on to describe old people's "sweetness" and other characteristics that did nothing to penetrate my stony heart. Fast-forward 30 years, and by the grace of God, I am right where Joan was back then. As I write this, my dear precious Auntie (the same one, bless her heart), is with us as she draws close to her 106th birthday. Her time in my home is ending, but she continues to lie in her bed day after day, using all her only slightly diminished brain power to conjure up new ways of convincing us to take her back to her home. Sometimes she gets the street wrong now, recalling the house of her youth. And sometimes she is very confused about where this strange room of her current residence is. *("I'm in trouble" she told a recent caller. "I'm in jail because I kidnapped my brother.")*

But despite, and sometimes enhanced by, the wandering of her still mostly lucid mind, I have a deep and tender love for my Aunt Margaret. When she's lying there cradling her stuffed baby doll, 'Marguerite', and she turns those bright eyes in that slender little face on me, toothlessly smiling oh so sweetly, my heart melts. And I can truly and most definitely see something so very extraordinarily beautiful in "old people". ❤

> **"I will give you a new heart and put a new spirit within you; I will take the heart of stone out of your flesh and give you a heart of flesh."**
> *– Ezekiel 36:26*

Margaret Amanda Chisley

June 26, 1911 – January 22, 2021
Rest in eternal peace and love.
Never Duplicated. Never Forgotten.

CHAPTER NINE

"An Unlikely Ally – Arachnophobia"

> *"Bear one another's burdens, and
> so fulfill the law of Christ."*
> *- Galatians 6:2*

So today, I met an unlikely ally in our garden. On my way to retrieve a tool from the shed, I walked into a spiderweb stretching between a tree and the garden fence. It must have been at least twenty feet long. As I watched, a giant spider scurried back to the safety of the tree branch and instantly curled up in a very successful attempt to camouflage itself. It looked like a very natural brown knot on the tree branch, making me wonder how many giant spiders lurked around me… (Giant might be a slight exaggeration, but suffice it to say that it would keep you awake if you encountered it in your house.)

I nervously proceeded into the garden enclosure and spotted another oversized spider on one of the squash plants. I had never seen spiders in or near our garden before and wondered about this new development. But my fear was stronger than my curiosity, so I went the other way and reported it to my husband. He investigated the matter and informed me a few minutes later that he had killed it.

When I returned to the garden, the Lord admonished me for killing the spider. He revealed that the spiders had been sent to fight off the insect pests that had destroyed our earlier vegetable crop. I had prayed for His help, never suspecting that protection would come in the form of these scary-looking creatures. They were eating the bugs that were ready to destroy our crops again. I instantly repented and asked Him to send more.

I believe there is an application to our Christian walk. Sometimes we find ourselves in situations or relationships that seem unsavory. Let's face it; some people just work our nerves. Have you ever considered ending a friendship because the person requires so much of your attention, patience, understanding, and spiritual and emotional resources?

You may have given godly advice to the person, which they followed for a time, only to revert to past bad decision-making. They don't fit into your plan, and they often reach out at the most inconvenient times. They may seem like undesirable intruders in your well-planned life. But perhaps the Lord has sent them to you for a reason.

This relationship you did not choose, just may be the Lord's choice for you. This is not to suggest that we remain in abusive, toxic relationships. I believe that we must seek and follow the Lord's guidance about every relationship, including platonic ones. But is it possible to have a mutually beneficial relationship with a person we would not consider as having any ability to benefit our lives? What they bring to your life may be something you never realized you needed.

Is it possible that the Lord is using this person to grow your compassion, self-control, generosity, or patience? Of course, you must set limits. As you seek the Lord's guidance, He'll identify the part He wants you to play. He'll even tell you when you need to withdraw in order to allow Him to work.

In the end, if you follow His lead and persevere, you will have served the Father's purpose in that person's life, and they will have served theirs in yours. And as you serve God's wounded people, don't be surprised if you discover a deep well of beauty in the person that had been hidden from your sight and maybe even from their own.

All of God's people are beautiful, regardless of the trauma that has brought them to the point of brokenness. It takes love for beauty to come to the fore. Just as the love of God has transformed us, so should we use the love He has given us to help others. And that beautiful, broken person can genuinely be your unexpected ally in growing more into the image of our beloved Savior, Jesus.

> **"A new commandment I give to you, that you love one another; as I have loved you, that you also love one another."**
> *– John 13:34*

CHAPTER TEN

"There Once Was a Tree"

> *"So the Lord said, "If you have faith as a mustard seed, you can say to this mulberry tree, 'Be pulled up by the roots and be planted in the sea,' and it would obey you."*
> - Luke 17:6

I've always loved trees and there are many on our property. Mostly wild but a few are cultivated. In that number, there are a couple that stand out from the crowd and make their own personal statement of beauty. One such tree stands alone in the middle of our backyard. In the spring it delights us with a beautiful display of white flowers. In the summer its lush green leaves are visible from most parts of the yard. This tree had always been one of our favorites.

A few years ago, the Lord impressed upon me that the vegetation that is on our land is our responsibility. He further impressed upon me that, for one thing, I should pray for the health of the trees. As I walked and prayerfully surveyed the property, I became concerned over the appearance of several trees, including this beautiful little tree. Upon close inspection, I saw that the black pod-like growths I had observed and pondered a few years ago had spread over the many branches both high and low. I immediately researched and located an arborist who would come and provide a free evaluation. (Shout out to Angie's List!)

A very tall (oddly tree-like I thought), young man came on that November morning, and as we walked the property, he seemed to demonstrate a vast knowledge and expertise. In most instances, rather than recommending expensive remedies to the numerous small problems he detected, he tended to minimize and even suggested self-help projects that we could do at little cost. But when he examined that particular tree, the news was not good. Black knot disease had completely overtaken the little cherry tree. His prognosis was that it's incurable, and that we should only remove and replace it.

As I was listening to his explanation and looking sorrowfully at the little tree, my eyes were drawn to something white. I stepped closer and detected a small white flower that had bloomed on a severely gnarled branch that appeared otherwise dead. When the arborist saw it, he stopped in his tracks – temporarily speechless. He had never seen such a thing in November, in Maryland. After a moment of stumped silence, he rationalized that it was further evidence that the poor confused tree was surely rendering its final siren call. But I pondered it in my heart.

When I mentioned it later to my friend, Joy stated that the flower was just evidence that God intended to heal the tree if I was obedient to His instructions. So, at the Lord's instruction, I proceeded to march around the tree seven times every day, praying for complete restoration.

Soon I saw several new green leaves sprouting on it. Praise the Lord for His Resurrection Power at work!!

But wait - it gets even better! The following summer we were absolutely delighted to discover that the little "cherry" tree, according to the tall arborist, was actually a plum tree that yielded the most delicious little plums which we discovered only after the deer had devoured those on the lower branches! SO glad we believed the report of the Lord!!

Whereas Matthew and Mark both saw fit to write about Jesus cursing the fig tree to demonstrate the power of faith, this is an object lesson for all who see the work of the Spirit in this situation. Jesus, our faithful Savior, and God's creative agent is truly the author and finisher of our faith! And it's such a blessing that He continues to build our faith day by day as we listen, trust, and obey Him!! All praises be to God!!!

> "Now faith is the substance of things hoped for, the evidence of things not seen."
> – *Hebrews 11:1*

CHAPTER ELEVEN
"Poor Purcell"

> *"Now I plead with you, brethren, by the name of our Lord Jesus Christ, that you all speak the same thing, and that there be no divisions among you, but that you be perfectly joined together in the same mind and in the same judgment."*
> *-1 Corinthians 1:10*

That's what my aunt called my husband - poor Purcell. I feel "some kind of way" about that nickname, especially since I think his marriage to me was the source of her pity. Humph!! But I must admit that life with me has not exactly been a crystal staircase.

Right now, as we sit at yet another real estate closing, I am reflecting on how I got to be a woman who buys and sells apartment buildings. Of course, it's all by the grace of God. This was never my plan - or even a bleep on my radar screen. I grew up living in apartments and never, in my wildest dreams, thought I would one day own them. Then I met and married Purcell.

I thank God for him - he has endured much over the past 28 years. Dragging me, kicking, and screaming from the comfort of my bi-weekly paychecks into the murky waters of business ownership has been no easy task. He is a man of vision, and I am a woman of security. Every new venture that he has enthusiastically presented to me has caused me to recoil at the thought of the risk involved. I like having a roof over my head and have steadfastly resisted any action that gives a bank the power to snatch it off!

But recently, the Lord has shown me that we must operate in agreement. Some of the losses we have suffered have been fueled by my negative attitude. He has given us another chance to succeed and thrive in true partnership. So here we are at another closing. To secure this property, we must relinquish all the savings we have accumulated from the sale of another building. From now on everything will be invested in the building that I never wanted to buy in the first place.

But I've decided to let God be God, and to let Him be our guide and provider. And as I sit across from the man God chose for me, I am committed more than ever to move forward in lock-step - loving, praying and working together to pursue what God has for us! No looking back! ❤

> "Again I say to you that if two of you agree on earth concerning anything that they ask, it will be done for them by My Father in heaven."
> *– Matthew 18:19*

CHAPTER TWELVE
"Pruning"

> *"And so we know and rely on the love God has for us. God is love. Whoever lives in love lives in God, and God in them."*
> - 1 John 4:16

Today I worked in our bed of Knockout Roses where much weeding needed to be done. Primarily, the weeds consisted of clinging vines intertwined in each bush. They were easily removed, but when I pulled them off, they exposed many brown, dead-looking branches in the plants. There were more healthy branches than dead ones, but even the healthy ones didn't appear to be thriving as much as they should be. My neglect had created a problem, and pruning was necessary. The dead branches needed to be removed so that the healthy ones could flourish.

As I worked carefully, the Lord began speaking about the pruning process that has already started and will be quickening in the Body of Christ. In John 15, Jesus talks about it in detail.

"I am the true vine, and my Father is the gardener. He cuts off every branch in Me that bears no fruit, while every branch that does bear fruit He prunes so that it will be even more fruitful." *John 15:1-2, NIV*

Saints, we are not exempt from this process. If we are producing fruit for God's Kingdom, we can expect to be pruned to produce more. If we're not bearing any, we will be cut off. While pruning doesn't sound like much fun, Jesus makes it clear in verse 6 that being cut off is much worse:

"If you do not remain in me, you are like a branch that is thrown away and withers; such branches are picked up, thrown into the fire and burned."

In my Knockout Rose Garden, the vinelike weeds, (external influences), though plentiful, had been easily removed. But the dead, unproductive branches within the plant also had to be removed, but more carefully. Thus, it is for the Church.

Yet, the Lord is ever merciful. As I was happily snipping away, He warned me to be careful. It was important not to harm the living branches as I cut away the dead ones. They were very closely connected in some cases, so caution was required. When I came to a branch that appeared to be dead, the Lord told me to look closer - to look for any sign of life. I looked very closely and finally saw the tiniest green leaf that was almost hidden from view. The Lord said to leave that branch intact but to carefully cut back the dead portions.

Our God is a careful gardener. He is patient, long-suffering, and kind. As He examines His Church, the plants in His garden, He will not snip away carelessly. He will give mercy to whom He will give mercy. (See *Romans 9:15*, **"For He says to Moses, "I will have mercy on whomever I will have mercy, and I will have compassion on whomever I will have compassion."**) His desire is for us to all be saved, to all produce good fruit. But judgment will begin first within the Church. (See *1 Peter 4:17*, ***"For the time has come for judgment to begin at the house of God; and if it begins with us first, what will be the end of those who do not obey the gospel of God?")***. It is up to us to choose the path to life, not once, but daily.

Have you ever considered that the five foolish bridesmaids in the Matthew 25 Parable may have had oil in their lamps the day or week before? Perhaps they had once been on fire for the Lord and for the things of His Kingdom. Perhaps they had gotten careless and let all their oil burn out without replenishing it. Jesus gives us the solution to this pervasive problem in the Church in verses 4 and 5 of the same 15th Chapter of John.

"Abide in Me, and I in you. As the branch cannot bear fruit of itself unless it abides in the vine, neither can you, unless you abide in Me. I am the vine, you are the

branches. He who abides in Me, and I in him, bears much fruit; for without Me you can do nothing."

This is not a suggestion but a somber warning that we would do well to heed. As we move closer to the return of our Beloved Savior, let Him find us doing what He asked us to do. Abiding – proactively ensuring that our connection to Him, the True Vine, is secure and strong. From that position of life-giving intimacy, He will give us the direction we need to produce plenty of good fruit for His Kingdom - fruit that the true Master Gardener cultivates in us for the purpose of nourishing others.

> "But the fruit of the Spirit is love, joy, peace, longsuffering, kindness, goodness, faithfulness, gentleness, self-control. Against such there is no law."
> – *Galatians 5:22-23*

CHAPTER THIRTEEN

"Not My Love, But Thine, Oh Lord"

> *"Dear friends, since God so loved us, we also ought to love one another. 12 No one has ever seen God; but if we love one another, God lives in us and his love is made complete in us.*
> *"*
>
> *-1 John 4:11-12, NIV*

For much of my life I have struggled with selfishness and self-centeredness. When I was a teenager, my brother called me 'stuck up.' He was trying to help me because he said, "Stop acting stuck up." As I recall, I was having some challenges relating to someone in our circle of neighborhood friends.

Nothing much changed since those days, even after becoming a Christian. With a few exceptions, I still lived primarily for myself. But God had a remedy lined up and waiting for me.

Enter Minister Regina Zellars, my friend, and one of the most generous and loving people I have ever known. Regina (a/k/a Gina) has a big heart and considers everyone she meets to be her daughter, son, sister, or brother. Gina walks the walk - day in and day out. She reaches out to those who others - even most Believers that I know - would reject at first sight. But Gina embraces, supports, and admonishes --in love. She is the real deal, and because of my friendship with her, I have had to step up to the plate to love unconditionally and assist, more times than I would have liked.

Each time I have done so, it's been with much resistance. My utmost desire has been to live happily ever after in my home with my family and an occasional visitor who doesn't need much of anything from me. (I'm keeping it real.) But the young people I have met since knowing Gina have all come from places of incredible brokenness and have needed more patience, love, and understanding than I ever thought I could muster.

The latest episode involved a single mother with a special needs child. Gina had mentioned them over the years and had enlisted our prayer team to pray with her for their needs. But now they needed something that I was in the best position to provide; they needed emergency housing, and I had the space. Because of Gina's connections and compassion, these types of needs are often presented to her, and she always reaches out to us to pray. At times she has mildly suggested that maybe I could be of help to the person. And I haven't had a problem helping, but only if it didn't require very much of me. Just a few months earlier there had been a bigger request - one that I had not granted, allowing selfishness to triumph. And here she was, knocking on my heart again.

My first impulse was to close my blinds and put up my "Gone Fishing" sign. But then I realized that was exactly what Gina was inviting me to do --to co-labor with her in being a Fisher of Men. She has often said, "They don't care how much you know until they know how much you care." So, this was an opportunity for me to show the love of God to His hurting children; a chance for me to walk the walk by sharing what He has given me - most undeservedly, with someone who had a real need and no way to repay.

Still, as I thought about the little girl Zoe, who had been acting out since her family's displacement, e.g., soiling herself on purpose, I couldn't imagine opening our home and exposing our nice furnishings to potential damage. My flesh strongly resisted as I put concerns for my possessions ahead of the real emotional, spiritual, and even physical needs of this young mother and child.

A tremendous struggle ensued, during which the Lord frequently coaxed me into our meeting room to help me to take the *right path*. As I made my case, reminding the Lord that He had just provided us with the new furniture, He simply said to me, **"You're going to love Zoe."** In other words, He wasn't really taking no for an answer.

I eventually gave in, and my husband and I consented to letting them stay with us for the few weeks they had requested. And Zoe was indeed a very lovable 10-year-old - even with her outbursts, awkward gait, and unpredictability. But she had an inward beauty that was expressed so clearly through her smiling eyes. I found myself loving her. My love also began to grow for her mom as I got to know her, and layers of selfishness began to slowly peel away - until the dog came.

She was not part of the plan. And even though she was a sweet, beloved pet and had nowhere else to go, I found the familiar spirits of selfishness and materialism returning with a vengeance. I was "fit to be tied," (i.e., very upset), and began to have serious second thoughts about the whole arrangement.

That night, I attended a church revival service, and the visiting pastor preached on love. Of course, he referred to *1 Corinthians 13:4-7*: "**Love is patient, love is kind. It does not envy, it does not boast, it is not proud. It does not dishonor others, it is not self-seeking, it is not easily angered, it keeps no record of wrongs. Love does not delight in evil but rejoices with the truth. It always protects, always trusts, always hopes, always perseveres.**" He spoke about how difficult it is for us to fulfill the requirements of love laid out in that chapter. I totally agreed. The type of love described in that chapter is beyond human capability - at least it certainly was beyond mine.

I listened closely to his message because I needed an answer. Towards the end, he brought us to a passage in Colossians: **"But above all these things put on love, which is the bond of perfection."** (*Col. 3:14*) and *Romans 5:5, (NIV):* **"And hope does not put us to shame, because God's love has been poured out into our hearts through the Holy Spirit, who has been given to us."**

My eyes were opened when he said that we cannot love others as we are supposed to with the love we received and were taught from our families. We **must** operate in the love that Christ *can empower* us with. That's a higher level of love - one that we must aspire to, but it is impossible in our own strength. After the service, I came home and prayed that God would provide me with His love so that I could love all the people He would place in my life, in His way.

The Lord answered my prayer, and both my husband and I were able to make our peace by continuing to support the growing family. Seven months later, our guests were stronger, healed, reunited with their precious son/brother, and ready to move into their own place. And I had a new little extended family to love; beautiful, imperfect people like me. We had to replace a few very small household items because of their stay, but the Lord had expanded my heart and my capacity to love His beautiful children. And their hearts have been joined with mine by our mutual connection to the Heart of all hearts. To God be all the glory!

"And hope maketh not ashamed; because the love of God is shed abroad in our hearts by the Holy Ghost which is given unto us."
– *Romans 5:5*

CHAPTER FOURTEEN

"That's It!"

> *"Delight yourself also in the LORD, And He shall give you the desires of your heart."*
> -Psalm 37:4

My husband was out of town, and I was encountering difficulties working on a project that I really needed to complete. As I was working on a particularly stubborn problem and feeling frustrated, I vaguely heard the Lord beckon me. It was very faint. I felt rushed for time, and I didn't want to stop my "important work". But He said it would be just a few minutes, so I walked quickly towards our meeting place.

As I was passing the front door and side windows, I saw a beautiful red autumn leaf on the porch, and as my eyes traveled further, I saw a large blue bird with soft, subtle but spectacular patterns on its wings, tail, and head. It was sitting in the flowerpot picking at something in the dirt. It was so close, and I could see every detail of the exquisite and precise design of its coat. I thought about how carefully the Lord had matched the colors and designs to put together the 'outfit' that adorned this magnificent bird. It stopped me in my tracks, and I stood there soaking in the unexpected vision of beauty. I knew that this was a treat arranged just for me by my precious Lord who I seemed to seldom find time for those days.

Watching that beautiful, perfectly decorated creature brought me a sudden peace as I reflected on the beauty of God's creation and His love in showing it to me - because I came when He called.

After a couple of minutes, the blue bird flew away, and I heard the Lord say, ***"That's it."*** In other words, this is what I wanted to show you. You can go back to your work now.

The Lord knows us. He knows what we love and wants to share it with us. He loves us in that way - deeply, personally, despite our sometimes-misguided notions and misplaced priorities. He wants us to draw close. He knows that we need to be refilled daily so that we can continue *to give*. That's it!

> "The Lord your God is with you, the Mighty Warrior who saves. He will take great delight in you; in his love he will no longer rebuke you, but will rejoice over you with singing."
> – *Zephaniah 3:17 (NIV)*

CHAPTER FIFTEEN
"A Simple Prayer"

> *"And I said, "This is my anguish;*
> *But I will remember the years of the right hand of the Most High." I will remember the works of the Lord; Surely I will remember Your wonders of old."*
> - Psalm 77:10-11

After a fretful night, we woke up in Kaiser's urgent care hospital room. My husband was still in a tremendous amount of pain and discomfort, and I was worried and upset. Seemingly, a doctor had previously botched a routine procedure. In frustration I had asked the Lord whether we should sue for malpractice. ***"Be at peace."*** was His response.

The urgent care doctors and nurses had tried unsuccessfully to relieve his distress and we had both been awake most of the night. Feeling helpless, sleep-deprived and with no end in sight, I decided to distract myself by browsing on my tablet. I came across an article entitled "Prayer Moves Mountains" by Dr. Tony

Evans. His testimony of God's miraculous provision in answer to a faith-filled prayer request reminded me of such an act on my behalf that occurred some years prior.

On the Saturday before Easter, our son Imari and I had gone to downtown DC to pick up our daughter Nia, who was riding the Megabus home from New York City. The bus was running very late, and we had been waiting forty minutes or more, parked in a "NO PARKING" space directly in front of the tiny storefront office. I wanted to get an update, and since there was no line at the counter, I reasoned that I could run in and out without risking a ticket. But when I returned to the car less than two minutes later, a meter maid was placing a $100 ticket under my windshield wiper. No amount of pleading would convince her to cut me any slack. As I climbed back into the car, my first impulse was to fuss and fume. Then I began to feel guilty when I recalled that a few days earlier I had committed to being a better financial steward. This was obviously a move in the wrong direction. But I believed that the Lord would forgive me and help me to honor my heartfelt desire. And when Imari said, "God will take care of this," I agreed and immediately felt at peace. The Megabus finally arrived a few minutes later. The next day was Easter; our dear daughter was home, and all was well.

Well, I paid for the ticket and forgot about the incident. After church the following Sunday, a member of our congregation handed me an envelope. She apologized because the Lord had instructed her to give it to me the week before - on Easter Sunday. Inside the envelope was a note saying, "The Lord woke me up and told me to write you this check. He didn't tell me why, but out of obedience, here it is." The check was for $100! On the very night that I received the $100 ticket, God had taken care of it by having her write me a $100 check! "Oh, how sweet to trust in Jesus!" *(And a big shout-out to Min. Lisa, who acted in obedience!)

Although it brings me joy to recall that incident now, it just created a small glimmer of hope on that morning in my husband's urgent care room. As I sat there, I heard the Holy Spirit say, *"A simple prayer prayed in faith."* He was prompting me to pray for the healing of my husband's body, but that day my faith felt weak. The Lord told me that I needed to spend time in His Word and He instructed me to get my Bible from the other side of the room.

On the way back to my seat I could tell that my husband was gearing up for another excruciating episode. The Lord said, *"Pray it,"* so I went to his bedside, laid my hand on his shoulder, and prayed, "Lord, please heal my husband." Then I proceeded to my seat to begin my reading. As I sat there, it dawned on me that the struggle my husband underwent was less severe this time. I hadn't heard the muffled groans that had accompanied his pain throughout the night. I asked him if he had experienced less pain, and with a sigh of relief he confirmed that he had. Thank You God! Everything shifted after that. The Lord brought us through, and my husband was on the road to recovery. The simple prayer prayed in (the size of a mustard-seed) faith had been answered! Hallelujah to our ever-loving and ever-powerful Lord and High Priest who always FAITHFULLY intercedes on our behalf, and He is forever finding ways to build our faith! JESUS is His Wonderful Name!

> "Now this is the confidence that we have in Him, that if we ask anything according to His will, He hears us. And if we know that He hears us, whatever we ask, we know that we have the petitions that we have asked of Him."
> *– I John 5:14-15*

CHAPTER SIXTEEN

"You Can Run, But You Can't Hide"

> *Let him turn away from evil and do good;*
> *Let him seek peace and pursue it.*
> -1 Peter 3:11

Lacey stirred, causing me to glance over just in time to see her sink deeper into the sofa cushions as she let out a deep sigh. She's at peace sleeping beside me.

Lacey is our daughter and son-in-law's beautiful 3-year-old Morkie pup. Earlier, she had been running wild. My husband had taken her outside without her leash because we couldn't locate it. Lacey had taken full advantage of her freedom - running enthusiastically throughout our yard. It's always a joy to behold. But when it was time to come in, she balked and decided not to come when called. Instead, she bolted in the opposite direction. My husband tried to get her, but each time he came close, off she went again. She continued these antics for some time.

Further attempts to uncover the leash were unsuccessful. I dug through her bag, hoping to find a treat to tempt her with. I found a new bully stick (a smelly chewy stick used as a dog treat.) The Lord said ***"Take that and sit on the front porch holding it out. She'll come to you."*** I did and Lacey ran straight to me. I scooped her up quickly and brought her inside.

Before I could give her free access to the house, she had to be cleaned up from her outside escapade. She reluctantly submitted as I sat her on a towel on my lap and proceeded to wipe her down. Afterwards, she received her treat and the bonus of lying beside me on the couch as I did my morning devotions.

Reflecting on the pup's morning, I see parallels concerning my life and my walk with the Lord. Sometimes I bolt off in the other direction when I feel overwhelmed by what He's asking me to do. There are times when I choose independence and self-indulgence. He unfailingly woos me back with His sweet persistence. Then, remembering that He knows what's best for me, I repent, submit, receive the cleansing I need through confession, and the reward of dwelling peacefully in His loving presence.

No matter how sweet independence seems for the moment, once we've experienced the deep fulfillment of His love, we can never stay outside of His will for too long. The only path back to peace is allowing our Lord to tame us. Then we can exhale and sink deep into the bosom of His faithful love.

PS. Recently I received this instruction from the Lord, which bears sharing. *"Come to Me when you feel overwhelmed or overburdened." You will from time to time; know that I understand. Just come and lay your burdens on Me. Don't hide. Because you know that I will find you, but time and opportunities will have been lost."* For me, that was a Selah! moment.

> **"Flee also youthful lusts; but pursue righteousness, faith, love, peace with those who call on the Lord out of a pure heart."**
> **– 2 Timothy 2:22**

CHAPTER SEVENTEEN

"Focus on What I Do Right."

> *"If then you were raised with Christ, seek those things which are above, where Christ is, sitting at the right hand of God."*
> - Colossians 3:1

I was running late for church as I left my driveway one morning. I had to wait for my neighbor to finish backing up before I could proceed. While passing in haste, I saw her nodding at me out of the corner of my eye. I had not even looked at her but was focused on my mission.

I felt strongly convicted for being a bad neighbor as I sped by. Jesus says explicitly that we are to love our neighbor, and how can I do that if I don't take the time to even know her? We'd lived in the house for four and a half years and had only seen each other on rare occasions and always from a distance.

Feeling guilty and disgruntled, I noticed how cold the car was on that blistery morning. I felt annoyed that my husband had not warmed it up as he usually does before leaving for church. I gladly turned my focus away from my own faults to what, at the moment, appeared to be my husband's.

In all fairness, we were both tired from hosting a party the night before for our drama cast, and my husband had also been running late that morning. But instead of counting my blessings that Purcell typically does this very thoughtful thing for me, I turned all my attention to this 'grievous oversight'. It felt like the most natural thing to do to look for a scapegoat so that I didn't have to focus on my own shortcomings. Then conviction set in.

I was very familiar with Jesus' teaching on specks versus planks in *Matthew 7:3-4*: **"And why do you look at the speck in your brother's eye, but do not consider the plank in your own eye? Or how can you say to your brother, 'Let me remove the speck from your eye'; and look, a plank is in your own eye?"**

So, taking my eyes off my husband's (tiny) speck, I began refocusing on the giant 'poor neighbor' plank lodged in my own eyes.

I knew guilt and self-condemnation weren't the proper focus either, but I wasn't thinking clearly. My emotions were in an uproar from being late, tired, cold, and frustrated. Then I found myself saying to the Lord, in a grumpy manner, "So You don't want me to focus on what *other people* do wrong, but only on what *I* do wrong?!" Jesus immediately responded, saying, **"Focus on what I do right."**

And there, in a nutshell, is the answer for me and you, dear reader. It's the answer to so many of life's dilemmas. Yes, we and others have flaws. Yes, we and others make mistakes. But when our attention is focused on the goodness of our marvelous and perfect Lord, His unfailing faithfulness, His loving kindness and tender mercies, and His undying love for us, our hearts have no choice but to be uplifted even as mine was in that instant! And then and only then will we be right where He wants us to be so that we can be transformed and made truly useful for His good purposes.

#ToKnowHimIsToLoveHIM!

> "You will keep him in perfect peace,
> Whose mind is stayed on You,
> Because he trusts in You."
> – *Isaiah 26:3*

CHAPTER EIGHTEEN
"Love THAT Neighbor!"??

> *But the fruit of the Spirit is love, joy, peace, longsuffering, kindness, goodness, faithfulness, gentleness, self-control. Against such there is no law*
> *– Galatians 5:22-23*

Our elderly family has a home in Virginia that no one is currently living in. My husband and I --primarily my husband -- have been working diligently to preserve the property following the flooding on two floors because of a burst pipe that occurred in late winter. Following the removal of flooring, drywall, and a major clean-up effort, we have gone by periodically to check on it.

It's a very old house, and while it is detached, the lots are narrow, and the neighboring houses are very close. On one side there is a narrow alley separating the two lots and on the other side there's only a fence. On one side we have a very nice neighbor who was very concerned, attentive, and considerate of the welfare of our elderly relatives when they were living there. The neighbor on the other side, however, has never displayed any awareness that there is another house three feet away, nor any warmth or consideration to our family. From the time he moved in, about five years ago, he has worked on building projects in his yard, starting early in the morning and going late into the night. He completely ignored my cousin's request to respect the fact that there were sick, elderly people living in the house, with ages ranging to well over a hundred years old.

One day we saw a notice on our family's front door announcing a zoning commission hearing on a proposal submitted by the not-so-friendly neighbor. He was requesting permission to build a two-story garage at the back of our adjoining lots. It was undoubtedly going to have a huge impact on the backyard visibility, light, and privacy of our family's property. My response was quick and indignant. My family had lived there for over 80 years, during which time we had enjoyed many family cookouts in the backyard. This new unfriendly neighbor was not going to destroy the peace and privacy of that backyard if I had anything to do with it! Humph!!

My husband's response was more restrained. And while I couldn't incite him to riot, he did agree that we should at least attend the hearing.

On the way to the hearing, I heard the Holy Spirit say**, "I don't want you to say anything. Purcell will be the spokesperson. Just sit there with a peaceful expression on** *your face."* This was hard for me to take because I wasn't sure that my husband would represent my outrage as well as I could. The Holy Spirit repeated, ***"I'm going to give you the victory. But Purcell is the spokesperson. You sit there with a peaceful expression on your face."*** Hmmm...

I made up my mind to obey since the Holy Spirit was so insistent. Still, several times I thought of things I could and wanted to say. Before the thoughts were fully formed in my mind, the Lord said firmly ***"Say nothing. I'm going to give you victory, but you must say nothing. Just sit there and look peaceful."***

I wasn't sure I could pull it off, but I also knew that it wasn't negotiable. So, I thought about one of the most peaceful looking members of my church, I'll call her Grace, and decided that I would imitate her expression.

Our neighbor's case was first on the docket. After the zoning commission introduced the particulars to those assembled, he called the neighbor up. I sat there imitating Grace's expression, being sure to keep the corners of my mouth turned upwards and trying to keep my eyelids from closing in a look of suspicious distaste. But while my expression looked calm and peaceful, my inside thoughts continued to rage. The Lord was ever faithful and patient, coaching me through by saying ***"Watch how I work this out for you."***

Purcell sat there calmly listening to the testimony, occasionally consulting the copy of the neighbor's paperwork that had been distributed. Finally, the neighbor took his seat, and the board opened the floor for questions and comments. Purcell raised his hand and was invited to come to the podium to speak.

He was very gentle in his approach, and was even cordial to the neighbor, turning to ask him a question from the podium. He then inquired of the board regarding a detail of the neighbor's diagram. After answering his question, the board chair asked him his opinion concerning the proposal. My husband calmly stated that our family was not in favor of the two-story structure, pursuant to the significant impact on the use and enjoyment of our yard. The board members all listened closely, and I saw several nods in agreement. I continued to sit with my peaceful expression.

I was beginning to see that the Lord knew what He was doing. Had I been the one speaking, I may very well have been banging my fist on the podium and shooting daggers at the neighbor out of the corner of my eye. The board probably would not have taken too kindly to my approach and may have even had me escorted out of the hearing room. Of course, my husband says that I would probably have dissolved into tears, which is what I often do when I'm upset. Not a pretty picture either way.

The Lord honored Purcell's gentle demeanor and gave us victory as He had promised. The Lord said, **"Gentleness will always be rewarded."** The neighbor's proposal was not approved, but God's victory was even sweeter than that! The board gave our neighbor permission to revise and resubmit his proposal, but only if he has a signed statement from my husband stating that our family approves of his revisions! The Lord set it up so that the unfriendly neighbor must reach out to my husband, giving Purcell a chance to demonstrate the love of God to a man who undoubtedly needs it like the rest of us. This decision changed the whole dynamic – turning the neighbor from an adversary to a God-assignment. To God be the glory!!

The board president referred to Purcell several times in discussing the board's decision, and now was further honoring him by recognizing him as the voice of calm reason – a man of integrity. True to His Word in Matthew 23:12, the Lord was exalting my husband because he had humbled himself.

Hallelujah and all praises to our All-wise, All-knowing, All powerful, most high, and Holy God who sits high and looks low, interceding in the affairs of men and women, and showing favor to His beloved children! He gave us victory that day, despite my initial hostile attitude. He proved once again that He loves us, even as we are. And He stands ready, always to demonstrate the better, more excellent way. Thank You, Abba Father. Holy, Holy, Holy are You, Lord God.

> **"The Lord will fight for you, and you shall hold your peace."**
> – *Exodus 14:14*

CHAPTER NINETEEN
"The Most Important Part"

> *"I will instruct you and teach you in the way you should go; I will guide you with My eye."*
> – Psalm 32:8

The alarm went off at 4:45 am. I'm not a morning person, so already the day was looking bleak. I had a dance ministry engagement two hours away and we had to be there by 8. After I hit the snooze button a few times, I had less than an hour to prepare.

My preparations included showering, attire selection, ironing and packing garments, making breakfast smoothies, and working on the choreography of my dance. One might ask why I hadn't done any of this beforehand. I would say it was a combination of over-commitment, poor planning, and lack of execution. Plus, I had gotten drenched the day before during a sudden downpour. As a result, I had to restyle my hair - a process which kept me up until very late the night before.

And now I had no choice but to rush around, frantically trying to get ready.

In addition, I was burdened with a nagging guilt over commitments I had left unfulfilled from the previous day. So, it's fair to say that I was totally unprepared to minister to God's people. In the middle of all this, as my husband silently watched to prevent me from getting sidetracked, I heard the Lord call me into the sanctuary. "Not now, Lord. I really don't have time." I said. Yep, that was my response! But He was gently persistent, so I went in without too much delay.

As I stretched out before Him, He started the conversation with, **"You do know that this is the most important part, right?"** And in that instant, I did. Indeed, coming before Him, confessing my sins, receiving forgiveness, instruction, and focusing... that was undoubtedly the most essential part of my preparations.

After that, everything got easier. I was able to complete all my preparations and we left on time. And I was able to turn my full attention to the assignment before me.

Today and every day, it is so important for us to prioritize hearing from the Lord on at least a daily basis. We all have many decisions to make every day. And while some of them may seem insignificant to us, God sees them differently.

As I reflect on God's perspective in comparison to ours, it occurs to me that there are no small things to the Lord. Everything has significance. He sees everything clearly for what it truly is. There's no nearsightedness or farsightedness – but perfect vision, perfect clarity, perfect understanding. Every small thing that would appear insignificant to us fits into a larger mosaic pattern and its significance is instantly seen and known - what that piece means for the whole and what the whole means for that piece.

And as for the things that we consider as nothing, well He knows that nothing is nothing and everything has significance, purpose, and carries weight in the larger scheme that He alone can see all at a glance fully and completely known and understood - past present and future. His vision is crystal clear and sharper than a laser beam. He knows the beginning from the end and everything in between. There's no confusion, no sense of being overwhelmed. It's all simple, clear, perfectly understandable. He can detect the smallest movement toward good or toward evil. Every instant in time holds significance for the coming future. It's a giant labyrinth of events and activities and beings and spiritual entities. Interplaying, interacting and interwoven in an infinite number of patterns and permutations, all of which He can observe at a glance.

And Holy Spirit is present with us who are Believers, boiling all the intricacies down to what an individual Believer should do or think or say at any instant in time.

As I reflected on this, the Lord asked *"And what does that mean?"* My answer to that - I should shut my big mouth, stop debating and resisting and just do what I'm told. Just be obedient. I'm learning. I say better late than never, and I'm thankful that the Lord has been so patient.

> "Seek ye the Lord while he may be found, call ye upon him while he is near: Let the wicked forsake his way, and the unrighteous man his thoughts: and let him return unto the Lord, and he will have mercy upon him; and to our God, for he will abundantly pardon."
> *– Isaiah 55:6-7 (KJV)*

CHAPTER TWENTY
"Tell Them About Me"

> *I thought it good to declare the signs and wonders that the Most High God has worked for me.*
> - Daniel 4:2

It had been an amazing day. I was enjoying a beautiful fellowship with the Lord as I drove into the city to take care of some business. Full of joy and peace, I parked the car and started to walk towards the building. As I turned the corner, I saw several people who appeared to be homeless sitting and standing in front of the entrance. Still as cheerful as ever, the Lord said *"Tell them about Me."* I felt a sense of trepidation at the thought, and responded, "Lord this is America. I'm sure they've heard about You." *"They haven't heard about Me from you,"* was His quick, still cheerful response.

As much as I love and enjoy my relationship with Jesus, I was content to keep Him to myself at that point. I wasn't excited about approaching a bunch of strangers and just starting up a conversation of any kind. My preference would be to just walk quietly by - perhaps with a quick nod in their direction. But there could be no doubt that this was the Lord making the request. And as much as I wanted to say no, how could I?

So, I girded up my loins as I approached the group, which included one very rough, rather scary looking woman. Very briefly, I spoke about Jesus to them. I told them how much He loved them. They appeared to be bored and barely listened, but I was just grateful that there had been no hostile backlash.

I breathed a sigh of relief and went into the building to complete my business. When I came back out of the building, I had expected to just walk back to my car. But before I could get away, the rough looking lady called me over. To my surprise, she wanted to talk more about Jesus, and I was able to share more of my personal testimony.

I pray that she and her friends will come to Jesus and receive His love for them. And I thank God for showing me the significance of our personal testimonies about Him. Our stories can help open the eyes of other lost souls who may unknowingly be looking for the same Savior who found and redeemed us. We're all the same on the inside, no matter where life's circumstances have taken us. We all need Him, and He passionately loves and wants each one of us.

"For we ourselves were also once foolish, disobedient, deceived, serving various lusts and pleasures, living in malice and envy, hateful and hating one another. But when the kindness and the love of God our Savior toward man appeared, not by works of righteousness which we have done, but according to His mercy He saved us, through the washing of regeneration and renewing of the Holy Spirit,"
– Titus 3:3-5

CHAPTER TWENTY-ONE
"COVID WOES"

> *Surely He shall deliver you from the snare of the fowler And from the perilous pestilence. He shall cover you with His feathers, And under His wings you shall take refuge; His truth shall be your shield and buckler.*
> *- Psalm 91:3-4*

I contracted Covid-19 in January of 2021. This was a surprise to me, because I had inquired of the Lord in March of 2020, and He had assured me that He would protect me and my family from Covid. So, when I got a positive test result, I was in denial until I tested a second time a few days later and received the same result.

I was confused, and wondered how I could have misunderstood His assurances. But here I was with two positive test results, and I had no choice but to quarantine in my home. My husband never contracted it and cared for me during the time of my isolation. I thank God that my symptoms were extremely mild.

During my isolation I enjoyed sweet communion with the Lord but was still confused about His promise. After eleven days, the county cleared me, and I decided to come out of quarantine without inquiring of the Lord. I was hungry, so in mask and gloves, I went to the kitchen to fix some food. While waiting for the toast, I went through the house checking things out while watering plants. I got all my food together and returned to the bedroom, surprised to find that I was feeling tired.

You see throughout the time of my isolation my symptoms had been mild and fatigue had not been one of them. I had taken 30-minute walks every day – either outside of the house or within the confines of my room. One day I walked for over an hour in the snow and had not gotten tired. But today, after less than 20 minutes in the kitchen, I began to feel weak. I went back to my room, got in bed and the fatigue quickly went away.

Finding myself hungry again in a couple of hours, I masked and gloved up again and went to prepare a quick snack. This time things immediately got worse. After just a couple of minutes I began to feel exhausted and had to hurry back to the bedroom. I went into the bathroom where I suddenly experienced a heavy, oppressive, sickening feeling crashing down over me. I felt that I could pass out from the sheer weight and magnitude of it and hastily sat down to avoid falling. I began proclaiming healing scriptures, rebuked the spirit of Covid, all to no avail. Then I heard the Lord say, ***"This is what I've protected you from."***

It felt absolutely life- threatening - something that I don't believe I could have recovered from. It went away as quickly as it came, leaving me physically, emotionally, and mentally shaken. It was absolutely the most horrible physical feeling I have ever experienced.

I made it back to the bed and as I sat there trying to collect myself, I heard a voice say

"Come back out and walk around the house. I want to show you my power."

I was scared to try and I just sat there in prayer asking God what to do. I heard "Go." I continued to pray. It wasn't until I said "Jesus, help me!" that I heard the Lord's voice say ***"Discern!"***

I knew then that it had been the enemy tempting me to go back out, so I stayed in the bedroom until the Lord instructed me to put on double masks and go outside for the daily walk with my husband.

We walked the entire 30-minute route at a brisk pace, and I barely felt it. I was dumbfounded and inquired of the Lord. He informed me that, for a reason that He did not disclose, I was protected outside of the house and in my room, but not in the rest of my house. If I went back out there before **He** released me (not the county, not the doctor) I would not be protected from the full, terrible impact of the virus. Furthermore, He told me that I was still contagious. That I should wear double masks and spray every time I open the door.

What I experienced briefly in the bathroom was something I wouldn't wish on my worst enemy – let alone my beloved family. I obeyed the Lord and remained in isolation until HE released me. My total quarantine time was 30 days, but I never experienced fatigue again and emerged completely healed with no lasting effects. My confusion about God's promise to protect me and my family from Covid had been cleared up. We each contracted it at some point during the pandemic, but every case was mild, Praise the Lord! My heart cries out HALLELUJAH!! Thank You God for saving us.

> **He who dwells in the secret place of the Most High shall abide under the shadow of the Almighty. I will say of the Lord, "He is my refuge and my fortress; My God, in Him I will trust."**
> *– Psalm 91:1-2*

CHAPTER TWENTY-TWO

"Persimmons"

> *"while, through the proof of this ministry, they glorify God for the obedience of your confession to the gospel of Christ, and for your liberal sharing with them and all men,"*
> *-2 Corinthians 9:13*

"What are those?" I asked my husband. We had seen two trees laden with a strange-looking orange fruit on our neighborhood walks over the summer and fall months. Neither of us knew what they were, but this is the story of how the Lord blessed me through one of these strange, exotic fruits.

My husband and I went to Costco last week. Our cupboards were quite bare and needed to be replenished. But our funds were a little tight, so I was consciously resisting the urge to 'stock up' for the future. The word "frugal" kept coming to mind. I did well until we came to the seafood department. My husband had been shying away from red meat and poultry, and since my vegetarian cooking expertise was rusty at best, we often found fish – particularly salmon – on our dinner menu. Salmon had become our family's number one go-to, fallback meal – especially since my husband had perfected his sautéed salmon filet recipe after learning to cook it during my lengthy Covid isolation. He loves to cook it, and we love to eat it.

I had been looking for a reasonably priced source for some time, and I was thrilled when I saw large bags of frozen wild caught salmon filets in the seafood freezer at Costco. I had never found them there before, and I eagerly grabbed an extra bag so we could have the comfort of knowing that there was more salmon waiting in the freezer.

As we continued our shopping, I heard the Holy Spirit say, ***"Give half away to someone who needs it."*** Of course, this would mean that we would only have half as much time before we would run out again. I decided that I would reason with the Lord so I silently responded, "But I don't even know who I could give it to." He quickly brought Zoe's mother to mind. So, I agreed, considering whether to go back and get another bag to replace the one we had to give away. I quickly dismissed the idea because the point was that I would willingly sacrifice something I wanted for the good of someone else. I understood, but still...

As we were finishing up our shopping trip, the last section was the produce section. Around the corner from the citrus and avocados, I saw a large crate of the orange fruit I had been wondering about (that we saw on our walk that day). The sign said that they were persimmons. I was very curious about how they tasted but I wasn't willing to purchase such a large quantity. I left Costco that day feeling a little disappointed.

I was scheduled to see the young lady that the Lord had brought to my mind in a couple of days, so I began to reason that I wasn't sure she even cooked salmon. The next day, I received a photo from her of some food she had cooked that day. I recognized the zucchini and squash and the rice but couldn't tell what the meat was. She told me that it was 'salmon and fish'. I get it, Lord. Sigh...

On the day that I picked Zoe up from the bus I cooked a nice meal which she really enjoyed. There was some of the meal left over, and I was happy to have a head start on our meal for the next night. But when I spoke with Zoe's mother, she reported having a headache because she hadn't eaten all day. So, I prepared a big plate with all the leftovers for her. The Lord reminded me of the salmon, so I gathered that as well. As I was packing it up with some extra water for them, I heard the Lord say, **"Good sharing, Cheryl."** That felt good! Too bad He has to still teach me to share at my age, but I'm glad He's willing to do it.

When she arrived to pick up her beloved girl, I was experiencing great peace and joy in my spirit. Zoe and I had so much fun together, and I felt good about sharing. It was like a vise around my heart had been removed. Joyfully I gave her the bags I had packed for her. She thanked me and then reached into her bag and said, "Here Aunt Cheryl. One of my coworkers gave me two of these today and I want to give you one. I've never seen them before. Do you know what it is?" My heart leapt for joy as I exclaimed "Persimmons!!!" Praise the Lord! He had once again shown His love in such a simple yet profound way. It brought satisfaction and peace to my heart, to once again be reminded that He's watching, He's listening, He cares, and He loves in such a precious way, and He has a sense of humor! My Jesus! My teacher and my friend!

> "Now the multitude of those who believed were of one heart and one soul; neither did anyone say that any of the things he possessed was his own, but they had all things in common."
> – *Acts 4:32*

CHAPTER TWENTY-THREE
"Snap, Crackle and Pop"!

> *"Is anyone among you sick? Let him call for the elders of the church, and let them pray over him, anointing him with oil in the name of the Lord. 15 And the prayer of faith will save the sick, and the Lord will raise him up. And if he has committed sins, he will be forgiven."*
> *– James 5:14-15*

I went into the sanctuary, barely able to breathe through the congestion in both of my nostrils. Headache, irritable throat, ears beginning to ache – the whole nine yards. Not Covid – just a bad summer cold. As I was lying before the Lord He asked, **"Do you want Me to heal you?"** I said "Yes!" I was miserable and afraid to stretch out because my nose was dripping like a faucet. He said **"Reach out and touch Me."** So, I stretched out fully and, in the Spirit, grabbed onto His feet. Slowly but surely, I felt my nasal congestion disappearing. Eventually my throat started feeling right. My head was still a little dull and I could still feel some pressure behind my eyes, but He said it would all clear up in a couple of hours. He told me to run some victory laps in the house and then to write about it and the other healing miracles I have experienced.

"You have to believe in My healing power, Cheryl."

I thought back to His healing of our son's premature puberty. When Imari was 3 years old, our daughter Nia's friend noticed that his legs were unusually hairy for a young child. She worked in an endocrinology office and excessive hairiness in early childhood is a symptom that is associated with a condition called premature puberty. I am not an expert, but premature puberty (now called precocious puberty) is when the child's hormonal balance is out of whack for their age and signals the brain to stop the growing process that normally continues until the end of puberty or until about age 20. In premature or precocious puberty, the presence of those hormones, normally present during the late teens or early 20s, causes a signal to be sent to the growth plates in the child's body to stop growing or something. Apparently, there are some bands at those joint locations that tighten. When that happens, growth stops. Our son was about 3 feet tall.

We were all very concerned and took him for hormone testing. While we were awaiting the results, I spent a lot of time in prayer, beseeching the Lord. I believed that He would give me His answer in church on Sunday.

I was running very late that Sunday and decided to go into the Fellowship Hall to watch the service. I was looking for an answer from the Pastor's message. But when I got into the Fellowship Hall, the TV feed wasn't working. My anxiety was already at an extremely high level, when my husband walked in and saw that the service wasn't being broadcast in that room which served as an overflow room at the time. I paced back and forth in fervent prayer as he went back to fix it. Suddenly it came on, right as my pastor said, **"Yet this is what the Sovereign Lord says: '"It will not take place, it will not happen …. If you do not stand firm in your faith, you will not stand at all.'"** (*Isaiah 7:7*).

To this day, I have no idea what else he said or whether he even filled in the dots in that scripture. What I heard, and what I remember is what I ascribed as the Lord's response to our fervent prayers: "It will not happen, it will not take place…stand on your faith or you will not stand at all." Hallelujah and Amen! I had my answer. It didn't matter what the hormone tests would reveal, God said it wouldn't happen, and I believed Him!

Imari slept in our bed that night, and I saw first-hand what God could do. Suddenly he awoke and grabbed his elbow and said "Ow. My elbow hurt." The pain went away quickly, and he went back to sleep only to awake again, grabbing his wrist saying "Ow! My wrist hurt." He drifted back to sleep and awoke a few minutes later saying, "Ow! My knee hurt." One by one, he was awakened from sleep by a sudden pain in each of his joints. The Lord was supernaturally breaking open or loosening the tightening that had begun to occur as his body had begun to shut down his growth.

Hallelujah! And Amen! The Lord was intervening in his body and preventing the stunted growth that would have occurred. Proof before my very eyes that God was healing our son in answer to our prayers and our faith! Jehovah Rapha had done as He promised and blessed me to witness Him at work!

Another time, during prayer service at our church, one of our ministers was complaining of debilitating migraines. As we joined hands and closed our eyes to pray for him, the Lord showed me a vision of a bolt of lightning traveling straight from heaven to the minister's head. He reported instant relief from his migraine pain. Praise the Lord for His awesome healing power!

Several years later, our daughter Nia called from Atlanta to announce that her mammogram had revealed a peach pit-sized lump in her breast. I immediately made reservations to fly down and accompany her to a follow-up appointment that week. I went to Gina's house, my friend and prayer partner, and asked for prayer. As Gina was praying, I felt something inside of my own breast pop. Fast forward, when Nia and I went to the specialist in Atlanta later that week they found nothing!! It turned out that the breast where I felt the pop was the same breast where the first doctor had found the lump. Hallelujah! Our God is faithful, and He is truly able! Thank You Lord for allowing me to witness Your healing power at work!

Saints, our God is the same yesterday, today and forever. He has the power; He is able, and He is willing to heal us and our loved ones. He wants us to believe, to receive and to share our testimonies - that faith would grow in the land and in our hearts.

> **"Heal me, O Lord, and I shall be healed;"**
> *– Jeremiah 17:14a*

CHAPTER TWENTY-FOUR

"Ain't Nobody Got Time for That!"

> *A person's discretion makes him slow to anger,*
> *And it is his glory to overlook an offense*
> *- Proverbs 19:11 (NASB)*

When it comes to taking offense, I am reminded of the words of the urban cultural legend, Kimberly "Sweet" Brown, who famously said: "Ain't nobody got time for that!"

While it may seem flippant, it is absolutely true! Our days are numbered. Our mortal lives have an expiration date. How tragic to leave this life only to discover that being offended robbed us of the joy, peace, and abundant life that the Lord came to give us. (John 10:10) Or that it robbed others of the benefit of the good works God had for us to do; assignments we couldn't complete because someone looked at us funny, or said something unkind? How tragic that, perhaps someone may even lose out on salvation, because we spent too much time nursing our wounds. They showed up for that divine appointment, but we didn't.

Offense takes our eyes off the prize - the mark of the higher calling of God for our lives. It turns us inward when our focus should be outward. It feeds our corruptible flesh.

My author friend Evelyn Wright once said that offense is presented to us like "tempting, fattening goodies on a silver party platter". Anybody hungry? But let us be wise and take note of the clawed fingers on the hand that is holding the platter – satan or his agents. And before we partake, we should check the ingredients.

For some of us, the main ingredient of the spirit of offense is pride. We get offended when we think we don't deserve the treatment we received. So, then we must ask ourselves, did Jesus deserve the treatment He received? Did He get offended? No!! He quickly forgave. ***Quickly*** - before pride or anger or bitterness could take root. Before He could be distracted from His mission, He rejected the plate offered to Him and chose not to be offended despite the torturous cruelty He endured.

The extent to which we take offense sometimes provides a good measurement of our spiritual state. Perhaps --just perhaps --we're thinking more highly of ourselves than we ought. **"For I say, through the grace given to me, to everyone who is among you, not to think of himself more highly than he ought to think, but to**

think soberly, as God has dealt to each one a measure of faith." *Romans 12:3* Sometimes when we believe we are walking in spiritual wholeness, offense can sneak up behind us.

During the pandemic quarantine, I had many thrilling encounters in the Word as the Lord opened my eyes to its beauty. In some ways I felt closer and more connected to the Lord than ever. I felt like I was on firm ground. Then one morning after a peaceful sleep, I was awakened by a text in which a contractor was implying, in a very gentle manner mind you, that I had not fulfilled a promise that I had made to her. I had in fact done what I said I would do before going to bed the night before. Immediately offense reared its ugly head in me. I was being falsely accused!! Rather than calmly and gently reassuring her, I quickly mounted my high horse of indignation.

"How dare she accuse me of neglecting her needs when I made certain to complete the task before I laid my head on the pillow!! Humph!! How dare she ..." Need I go on? I was officially offended. Though I was being fed daily by the Word of God, I had quickly fallen into a trap without giving it a second thought. *1 Corinthians 10:12* soberly warns us, **"Therefore let the one who thinks he stands firm [immune to temptation, being overconfident and self-righteous], take care that he does not fall [into sin and condemnation].** *(Amp)* Truer words have not been spoken. I had taken a big bite out of the delicious looking, poisonous delicacy on the silver platter that had been waiting for me when I opened my eyes.

Thankfully I caught myself before turning a harmless situation into a seriously scrambled mess. I remembered what my friend Evelyn had said, and the lessons I had been learning. After reading the 1 Corinthians verse above, the Lord had said to me *"**Be warned! Don't just pay lip service, but truly be warned. There are MANY dangers out here for you. Pay close attention to your heart and your motives daily.**"* I quickly repented to God, asked for forgiveness, and forgave the one whose innocent question had sparked such a violent fire in my heart.

As the Holy Spirit warned, God's Word is to be taken seriously and applied personally because indeed, He knows what awaits us, and He is fully committed to our successful journey. This misstep was relatively minor, but the next one could have dire consequences. Thanks be to God that He is ever-present and all-knowing. But let's not forget that He also admonishes us to be alert in order to avoid the enemy's traps. **"Be sober, be vigilant; because your adversary the devil walks about like a roaring lion, seeking whom he may devour."** *1 Peter 5:8*

We have entered a season of acceleration in God's Kingdom. He is preparing us - moving us into place for His mighty move upon the earth. Let's not let offense snuff out our lamp, making us like the five foolish virgins in Matthew 25 who weren't ready to move with the bridegroom. Let's decide that from this point forward, with God's help, we won't fall into that trap. Let's pray for a heart that will be unoffendable! Through Christ, we can do all things!

> **"Behold, I send you out as sheep in the midst of wolves. Therefore be wise as serpents and harmless as doves."**
> *– Matthew 10:16*

CHAPTER TWENTY-FIVE

"Left Behind"

> *"And at midnight a cry was heard: 'Behold, the Bridegroom is coming; go out to meet him!' Then all those virgins arose and trimmed their lamps. And the foolish said to the wise, 'Give us some of your oil, for our lamps are going out.' But the wise answered, saying, 'No, lest there should not be enough for us and you; but go rather to those who sell, and buy for yourselves.' And while they went to buy, the Bridegroom came, and those who were ready went in with Him to the wedding; and the door was shut.*
>
> *"Afterward the other virgins came also, saying, 'Lord, Lord, open to us!' But He answered and said, 'Assuredly, I say to you, I do not know you.'*
>
> *"Watch therefore, for you know neither the day nor the hour in which the Son of Man is coming."* – Matthew 25:6-13

Friends,

Today it's harder than ever but more important than ever for us to keep our lamps full of oil. Those of you who are Believers know the ten bridesmaid's parable that Jesus taught in Matthew 25. When He, the Bridegroom arrived He found ten maids waiting, but only five had enough oil for their lamps. He took the five and left the others to perish. Note that they were all waiting for His arrival, but only half were prepared.

Jesus is coming back. No one knows exactly when, but everything in our world seems to indicate that it will be soon. Of course, every generation since the first century has believed His return to be imminent. Still, there can be no denying that that day is closer than ever before. And our personal departure time from this earth may come even sooner than His return.

God wants all of us to be saved. To be prepared to enter into His eternal glory. So how can we be prepared? In *Matthew 24*, Jesus makes this statement about the Last Days - **"Because of the increase of wickedness, the love of most will grow cold, but the one who stands firm to the end will be saved."**

Can the lack of oil signify insufficient love for the Lord and others? Is the increase of wickedness - and maybe our allegiance to and acceptance of sin, be causing our love for the Lord and others to grow cold? Now is the time to examine our hearts - to seek the Lord for an honest assessment. If He returned tomorrow or your life ended tomorrow, would you enter His rest or be left outside like the unprepared bridesmaids? Will you be ready, and if not, what do you need to change?

Remember, all ten bridesmaids expected to enter the wedding feast. But five couldn't. We must purpose in our hearts and set our will to make any necessary adjustments. Repentance and personal accountability to righteousness may be necessary. Praying for us all.

> "I beseech you therefore, brethren, by the mercies of God, that you present your bodies a living sacrifice, holy, acceptable to God, which is your reasonable service. And do not be conformed to this world, but be transformed by the renewing of your mind, that you may prove what is that good and acceptable and perfect will of God."
> *– Romans 12:1-2*

CONCLUSION

"An Uphill Climb to The..."

> *"When I said, 'My foot is slipping,' your unfailing love, Lord, supported me."*
> *– Psalms 94:18 (NIV)*

Growing up, my neighborhood friends and I always had to have the latest 45s and loved to have house parties and "get-togethers" where we would dance for hours on end. I enjoy most of the old rhythm and blues songs - even those that are relatively obscure and unknown. I know I'm dating myself, but does anyone remember the 1966 Walter Jackson song entitled "An Uphill Climb to the Bottom"?

This morning, after waking up and spending time with the Lord, I began to reflect on my pilgrimage with Him. It's been almost 30 years since I came to know and love Him, but often it seems that I am stuck repeating the same cycles. In my battle to crucify my flesh I find that after my greatest victories there's a powerful resurgence of my flesh that I seem to succumb to far too easily.

He always sends His Spirit to coax me back to my feet and keep me from wallowing in self-condemnation. He's such an encourager, and always, unfailingly does His part to keep me going. But though He doesn't condemn me, I feel so disappointed in myself. As I reflect on all that He has poured into me, I wonder why I can't do better - why I can't withstand temptation more effectively. I feel that I have disappointed Him yet again. I want Him to be proud of me...though not quite as proud as He was of Job - if you know what I mean. . .

So, after a time of repentance and fellowship, the Lord encouraged me to come and work on my book. After reading a couple of previously written chapters, this title came to my mind. "An Uphill Climb to the..." After disappointing myself and presumably the Lord, it feels like I must climb back up to the starting blocks - from the bottom, as it were. But as I'm writing this, He's giving me pause to consider whether that is actually the case.

As I look back at the challenges I have had in growing to be more like Christ, I can see some progress. Some of the people I have considered to be difficult in the past, I'm now finding it within my capacity to love, and I desire to work for what is good for them. I couldn't do that in the past - never even had a desire to. I'm finding that I have allowed the Lord to soften my heart, and to enlarge my capacity to love. That is no small victory, and it is enduring! Even when I have those moments when my desire for comfort and ease in my life trumps my concern for others, Jesus turns around and plays the BIG JOKER OF LOVE on my little joker of SELF! And there I am, a step closer to Him, another step away from selfishness and selfish ambition.

So yes, it is an uphill climb beloved friend. But as we allow Him to work on us, and to lead us, we're not headed back up to the *bottom*, but up to the top! Up to where He wants us to be! HIS love will continue to relentlessly lift us up to where we belong - right by His ever-loving side!! OH, HOW I LOVE JESUS!!! ❤❤❤

> **"Now to Him who is able to keep you from stumbling, And to present you faultless Before the presence of His glory with exceeding joy, To God our Savior, Who alone is wise, Be glory and majesty, Dominion and power, Both now and forever. Amen."**
> *- Jude 1:24-25*

ADDENDUM
"Hearing His Voice"

God wants to speak to you. You are His beloved child, and He wants to have a close and intimate relationship with you. In *John 4:23-24*, while speaking to the Samaritan woman, Jesus says: **"But the hour is coming, and now is, when the true worshipers will worship the Father in spirit and truth; for the Father is seeking such to worship Him. God is Spirit, and those who worship Him must worship in spirit and truth."** Hearing from God is not a mental exercise, it is a spiritual encounter.

As Believers, we have been given spiritual ears through the presence of the Holy Spirit. As your life progresses, there will be many times when you need to hear His voice, as I do. At the beginning of my Christian walk, I was blessed to sit under the teachings of an anointed pastor who taught about the personal relationship that God desires. This awakened within me the faith to believe as well as a strong desire to hear from Him, our God. One would have to ask who would not want to commune with our blessed Savior who loves us with a consuming love? He knows us fully and always has our best interests at heart. All-wise, all-knowing, all powerful, yet humble and gentle. The popular saying comes to mind "It's not what you know, it's who you know." There is no one more worth knowing than our loving Savior.

In *John 10:27*, Jesus says **"My sheep hear my voice and I know them and they follow Me."** If we are His followers, we are supposed to hear His voice. Hearing Jesus' voice is part of our inheritance and a precious gift that we should desire. We hear His voice when we read His Word and He quickens it in our re-created human spirit. We can also have personal, one-on-one conversations with Him as He steers us through our daily lives; as He soothes our aching hearts as He teaches us and transforms us into His beautiful likeness. He is available to each one of us! Why would any of us consider settling for less than what He has made available to us? He gives it because He knows we need it.

The Lord spoke the following to me recently. *"**I speak to you because you come to Me expecting to hear. Tell others to do the same. I'll do the same for all of them. Add that into your book. Make it clear and plain.**"*

As with every one of His blessings, the first step to hearing from God is faith. Expect that He will speak to you. If you're a born-again Believer and you're having difficulty hearing, I recommend that you try the following:

- Purchase a notebook or journal that you will commit to using *only* during your time with God.

- Schedule a set time every day to go into your Prayer closet with your journal.

- Separate yourself from everyone and every distraction. Ask the Lord to speak to you however He desires.

- Sit quietly and write whatever thoughts and ideas come to you. Don't try to think of things to write. Just be receptive to hearing from the Lord. Playing quiet worship music may help you to relax and focus on Him.

- The next day, read what was written. Check to be sure that what you wrote is not contrary to His revealed will or character in scripture. The Holy Spirit will give witness as to whether this is a true Rhema word from the Lord.

- If you're still not sure, check with your spiritual covering for encouragement and confirmation.

I encourage you to make this a priority. His counsel is priceless. It is of inestimable value. As you begin to hear from Him more regularly, you will get to know Him better and to love Him more.

Seek Him because He's beautiful. Seek Him because you need Him. Ask Him to give you the faith and the desire and the will. In closing, I offer this simple prayer for you, beloved readers:

Dear Lord,

You are my Savior, You are my keeper, You are my provider and my sustainer, You are my deliverer, my healer, my comforter, and so much more. I believe, based on Your written Word, that You desire to commune intimately with me and to lead me by Your Rhema Word. I believe that You speak to me and desire that I would seek to hear. I ask that You increase my faith and strengthen my desire. Remove all fear and doubt and help me to enter a new level of intimacy with You. Teach me how to listen Lord. In Jesus' name I pray. Amen.

Beloved, if you prayed that prayer with sincerity the Lord will grant your desire. It is in perfect harmony with His desire for you. The above steps were given to me to share with a dear family member. I pray that they help you to begin the great adventure of communing directly with our Lord. If not, or if you want to go deeper, there are excellent books on hearing from God. I suggest that you purchase and read them for greater insight.

As we press in through praise and worship and prayer – especially in your prayer language, the Lord will make His presence known to you. He will speak because it is His desire to be your shepherd on a daily basis. Open your heart and spirit to Him and you will find yourself in blessed and sweet communion with the lover of your soul. I believe you will find what your heart and your soul have been longing for.

> *"As the deer pants for the water brooks,*
> *So pants my soul for You, O God."*
> *– Psalm 42:1*

> *"Then [with a deep longing] you will seek Me and require Me [as a vital necessity] and [you will] find Me when you search for Me with all your heart."*
> *– Jeremiah 29:13 (AMP)*